DINOSAURS
OF NORTH AMERICA

DINOSAURS
OF NORTH AMERICA

by HELEN RONEY SATTLER
illustrated by ANTHONY RAO

With an introduction by Dr. John H. Ostrom,
Curator of Vertebrate Paleontology,
Peabody Museum of Natural History, Yale University

LOTHROP, LEE & SHEPARD BOOKS / NEW YORK

Acknowledgments

I would like to express my deepest appreciation and thanks to John H. Ostrom, Curator of Vertebrate Paleontology, Peabody Museum of Natural History, Yale University, for reading the completed manuscript and adding many valuable comments and criticisms, and for checking the drawings for accuracy.

I also extend thanks to James H. Madsen, Jr., Wann Langston, Jr., James Jensen, Glen J. Ungerman, Denny Davies, and Lynn Loetterle for their contributions by way of conversations or correspondence. To the following authors for information gleaned from their papers published in scientific journals: R. M. Alexander, Robert T. Bakker, M. K. Bret-Surman, Adrian J. Desmond, Peter M. Galton, Stephen Jay Gould, Alan Hagood, John Horner, Wann Langston, Jr., James H. Madsen, Jr., John S. McIntosh, Ralph Molnar, William J. Morris, John H. Ostrom, Dale A. Russell, William Lee Stokes, John E. Storer, R. A. Thulborn, and Samuel P. Welles. To Robert Sattler, Carol Winfield, and Judith Furlong for their tireless assistance in finding reference material, to Alice Gilbreath for checking for grammatical errors, and to Peter Sattler, who inspired me to write this book.

Library of Congress Cataloging in Publication Data

Sattler, Helen Roney.
Dinosaurs of North America.
Bibliography: p.
Includes index.
SUMMARY: Discusses more than 80 different types of dinosaurs native to North America in the context of changing geography, animal and plant communities, and climate during the Mesozoic Era.   1. Dinosaurs—Juvenile literature.   2. Paleontology—Mesozoic—Juvenile literature.   3. Paleontology—North America—Juvenile literature.   [1. Dinosaurs.   2. Paleontology]   I. Rao, Anthony.   II. Title.
QE862.D5S22   567.9′1′097   80–27411   ISBN 0–688–51952–0

CONTENTS

Introduction

Few subjects intrigue the young (and the old) as much as do the dinosaurs. Many books have been written about the wonders and inexplicable natures of these giant saurians (dragons) of the past. But Mrs. Sattler's book is the first devoted exclusively to the dinosaurs that were native to North America. Thoroughly researched, it includes all of the kinds that have been discovered so far.

Mrs. Sattler reviews these Mesozoic North Americans in the context of a changing, dynamic earth—one of changing environments, changing geography with drifting continents, and changing animal and plant communities. This readable and enjoyable book brings back to life the very different world of the distant past—with its exotic and spectacular creatures.

John H. Ostrom
Curator of Vertebrate Paleontology
Peabody Museum of Natural History
Yale University

What Is a Dinosaur?

Millions of years ago, dinosaurs may have browsed where you now live. Dinosaurs roamed North America, just as they did other continents of the world. The word "dinosaur" means "terrible lizard," but dinosaurs were not lizards, and not all of them were terrible. Maybe they were not even reptiles. Reptiles are cold-blooded animals like lizards and snakes. Scientists used to think that all dinosaurs were cold-blooded. Now, many scientists believe that at least some dinosaurs developed a step beyond reptiles and were warm-blooded. This means that their bodies did not cool off when the temperature dropped.

Many people think dinosaurs were huge, slow-moving, ferocious animals that weren't very smart. That is not a true picture of what dinosaurs were really like. Some were fierce, but most dinosaurs were harmless, peaceful animals. Although some were giants—like "Ultrasaurus," which may have been taller than a five-story building, 100 feet (30 m) long, and weighed 80 tons (72 metric tons)—some were half the size of a chicken. Some were slow, but others may have been capable of running 40 miles (65 km) per hour. And many dinosaurs were probably not as dumb as people used to think.

Two kinds of animals are called dinosaurs. The two kinds were no more closely related than turtles and alligators. One kind had lizardlike hips and the other had birdlike hips. However, both lived within the same time period. The time when dinosaurs lived is called the Mesozoic (mez-o-ZO-ik) Era.

The Mesozoic Era started about 225 million years ago. The last dinosaur died about 65 million years ago, long before any humans were born. Sixty-five million is such a huge number, it is hard to realize how long ago that was. But you can get some idea. If you started right now and counted day and night without ever stopping, it would take you a little over two years to count to 65 million.

North America today is very different from what it was in Mesozoic times. At the beginning of the era, all of the earth's land was clumped together into one huge supercontinent. What is now North America was a part of that supercontinent.

Many different kinds of animals lived during that time. One kind of animal, the dinosaur, was more numerous and more important than the others. Just as humans are dominant today, dinosaurs were dominant during the Mesozoic.

Scientists have divided the Mesozoic Era into three periods. These are called the Triassic (try-ASS-ik), the Jurassic (jur-ASS-ik), and the Cretaceous (kre-TAY-shus). North America underwent many changes during each of those periods. The size and shape of the land changed. The climate changed, and the plants and animals changed.

Different kinds of dinosaurs lived here during each of those periods. We know this because they left traces such as bones, teeth, footprints, or skin impressions that have petrified, or hardened into stone. These are called fossils.

We don't know how many dinosaurs there were, because we only know about those whose fossils have been found. For every dinosaur that left fossilized traces, there were many more that did not. Fossils formed only when the animal's body was covered by deep layers of mud or sand soon after it died. The soft part of the body rotted away; only the bones remained. Over millions of years, mineral-rich water seeped through the mud, sand, and bones, turning them into stone and preserving them for us to find and study.

Fossils of more than three hundred kinds of dinosaurs have been found in all parts of the world. Not all kinds have been found in North America. However, since all of the continents were connected during the Mesozoic Era, it is possible that every kind lived on our part of that supercontinent at some time, and that scientists just haven't found the fossilized traces yet.

Scientists who study fossils are called paleontologists. They have found fossils of more than eighty different kinds of dinosaurs in North America, and new kinds are still being discovered. There may be thousands yet to find.

Not all of the North American dinosaurs lived at the same time, and no species lived through the entire age of the dinosaurs. As conditions became unsuitable for one species, it died out and another took its place. From old kinds, new ones developed with adaptations that made them better suited to their surroundings. Each new species of dinosaur was a little different from its predecessor.

No person ever saw a live dinosaur, because they had died out long before there were people on earth. We only know they existed because we have found their fossils. From dinosaur skeletons we can see how large they were and how many toes or "fingers" they had. Scientists also know how and where the muscles were fastened to the bones. From fossilized skin impressions, they can tell what the skin of some dinosaurs looked like. And they know by the kind of teeth a dinosaur had whether it ate plants or meat.

The first dinosaurs appeared about the last third of the Triassic period. By the end of the Cretaceous period, all of the dinosaurs had died out and the land had split into the continents we know today.

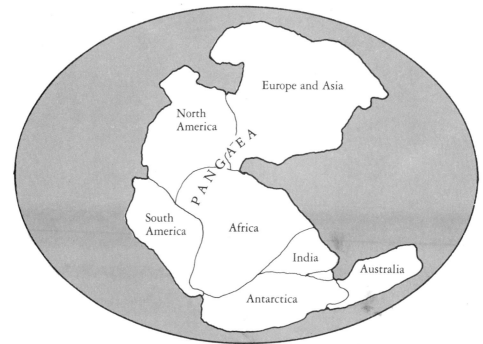

Triassic world
190–225 million years ago

Late Cretaceous world
65–100 million years ago

At the beginning of the Mesozoic Era, all the land areas on earth were connected in a supercontinent, which we call Pangaea. This supercontinent gradually broke up and drifted apart. The last map shows the continents as they are today.

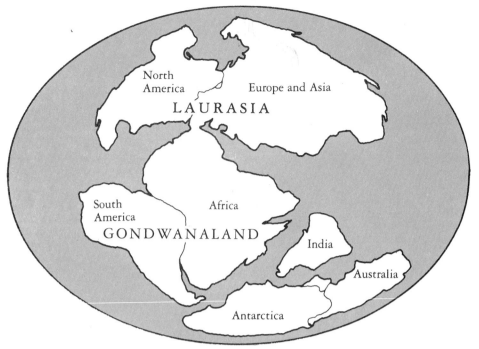

Jurassic world
140–190 million years ago

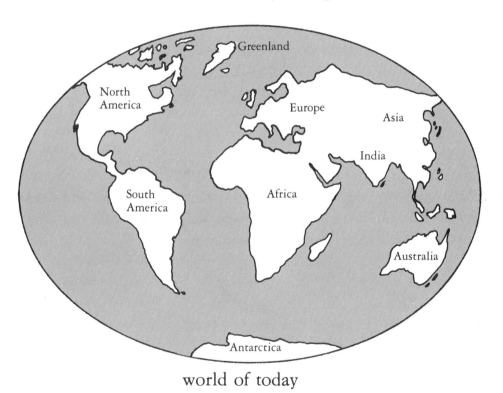

world of today

2

The Triassic, a Time of Change

A visit to our continent in the days of the Triassic period would have been like a visit to another planet. The Appalachian Mountains were there, but they would have looked more rugged, like the Rockies of today, because they were newly pushed up. The rock that makes up the Palisades of the Hudson River was just being formed from the lava of the many active volcanoes that could be seen along what is now the eastern coast.

Of course, there was no Atlantic seacoast at that time, because during the Triassic this was in the middle of the supercontinent and was a hot, often dry region peppered with many large lakes. Instead of an ocean, vast stretches of land reached thousands of miles eastward. Today, this land is known as Africa.

Little is known about the central part of North America during the Triassic period. Very few outcroppings of Triassic rock are found there.

However, we know much about the western part. What is now the West Coast was covered by ocean. Some areas of the West were swampy jungles; the land was low and flat. There were a few volcanoes, many lakes, large, slow-flowing rivers, and dense tropical plants and trees. The rivers had wide valleys that often flooded, laying down deep layers of sand and silt. The Painted Desert of the American Southwest was formed by those rivers.

Other parts of the Southwest were semiarid uplands covered with pines. Occasional violent cloudbursts washed fallen tree trunks downstream, where they were covered with sand and silt and fossilized. Today, those ancient tree trunks can still be seen in the Petrified Forest of Arizona.

The climate was mostly warm and humid even in Alaska and Greenland, which were much farther south than they are today. The temperature

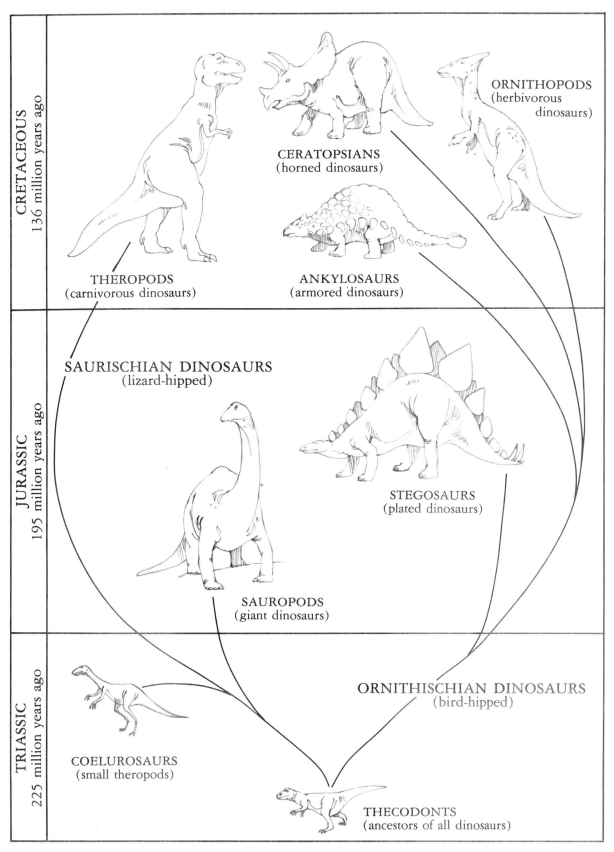

The evolution and classification of the dinosaurs, shown on a simplified "family tree."

seldom rose very high or dropped very low, and there were frequent rainfalls. These conditions were ideal for the development of huge animals.

Enormous 20–30-foot (6–9-m) Rutiodons (crocodile-like reptiles), small mammal-like reptiles, and 8-foot (2.5-m) amphibians dominated the land. Dinosaurs were present, but only a few fairly small Triassic dinosaurs have been found in North America. Scientists believe there were many more—they just haven't been found yet. They may never be. Triassic animals were buried in rock that is now several miles deep or already eroded away. Only in places where this rock has been pushed up by vast earth movements and the top layers washed or worn away are Triassic animals found.

These first dinosaurs looked very much like their ancestors, the thecodonts. Thecodonts were reptiles (like present-day snakes, lizards, and crocodiles), but they were different from other reptiles. They had light, thin, and sometimes hollow bones. Their front legs were short, but the hind legs were long and strong. A few thecodonts may have run on their hind legs the way some modern lizards do. Some ate meat; others ate plants. Unlike most reptiles, they had teeth set in sockets. Large numbers of thecodonts roamed North America and other parts of the world during the first half of the Triassic period.

LIZARDLIKE HIP
(saurischian)

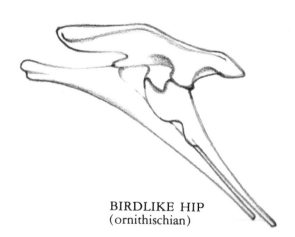

BIRDLIKE HIP
(ornithischian)

Triassic Dinosaurs

Although both kinds of dinosaurs—those with lizardlike hips and those with birdlike hips—lived in other parts of the world during this time period, only lizard-hipped dinosaurs have been found in Triassic North America. Lizard-hipped dinosaurs are called **saurischia** (sawr-ISS-kee-uh). There were two kinds of saurischian dinosaurs. The two-legged meat eaters are called **theropods** (THER-uh-pods). Four-legged plant eaters are called **sauropods** (SAWR-uh-pods).

Coelurosaurs
"Hollow Lizards"

The earliest dinosaurs that have been found in North America were small theropods. They belonged to a class called coelurosaurs (see-LURE-uh-sawrs). From their fossilized bones and footprints we know that they had slender legs, long necks, small heads, long tails, and hollow bones. We know by their sharp, notched teeth that they were meat eaters. The largest North American Triassic coelurosaur was 6–10 feet (2–3 m) long. Others were quite small.

All coelurosaurs had short front legs and grasping fingers. They walked on their strong hind legs, which had long toes. Footprints left by coelurosaurs in sand and mud look like large bird tracks. Although they had lizardlike hips, these animals were very birdlike in some ways.

Coelurosaurs were very successful dinosaurs. There was at least one living species of coelurosaur in every period of the Mesozoic Era, the entire 140 million years of dinosaur history. Some of the coelurosaurs' relatives may still be alive. Many scientists believe that coelurosaurs were the ancient ancestors of birds. Coelurosaurs may also have been the ancestors of the giant meat-eating dinosaurs.

Four kinds of Triassic coelurosaurs have been found in North America: *Coelophysis, Podokesaurus, Spinosuchus,* and *Segisaurus.*

COELOPHYSIS
"Hollow Form"

Coelophysis (SEE-lo-fise-iss) is one of the oldest known dinosaurs of North America. This large coelurosaur appeared early in the last half of the Triassic. Like all coelurosaurs, *Coelophysis* walked on two long hind legs with a long, slender, whiplike tail held out behind.

From the tip of the nose to the tip of the tail, this dinosaur measured between 8 and 10 feet (2.5 and 3 m). It stood about 3 feet (90 cm) at the hips. It weighed only 100–150 pounds (45–68 kg) because its thin, delicate bones were hollow. That is how it got its name. This graceful animal must have looked like a huge bird without feathers. Instead of feathers, it probably had leathery, scaly skin like an alligator's.

Coelophysis had a long neck that held its head high above the ground. Its large eyes could keep a sharp lookout for its enemy, the phytosaur, a huge, crocodile-like reptile that lived in the streams. However, its best protection was speed. *Coelophysis* was capable of running very swiftly. Its three-toed feet left 5-inch (12.5-cm) birdlike footprints in the Triassic mud and sand.

Coelophysis's front legs were short. The hands had three long fingers and one very short finger. They could easily hold the prey that was caught in the sparse underbrush of ferns, horsetails, pine trees, and palmlike shrubs. *Coelophysis* probably ate small amphibians, lizards, rat-sized mammals, scorpions, and insects such as ants, termites, cockroaches, and dragonflies.

Coelophysis might have hunted in packs. In groups these animals could have attacked larger, plant-eating dinosaurs. Their long jaws were filled with many thin, bladelike teeth that had serrated edges, like a steak knife—excellent for catching meat and slicing it.

Large numbers of *Coelophysis* lived in what were then dry upland regions. Hundreds of dinosaur footprints have been found in what is now the Connecticut River Valley. Some of these may have been made by *Coelophysis.* Scientists believe that *Coelophysis* lived in herds. This theory is supported by the discovery of skeletons of whole families together in New Mexico. This find also suggests that these dinosaurs may have taken care of their young.

Some scientists think that these dinosaurs were as mentally alert as

Coelophysis

phytosaurs

Coelophysis *and its reptilian enemy, the phytosaur.*

birds, and that they must have been warm-blooded because they were very active and agile. *Coelophysis* probably laid small eggs, although some scientists think they may have given birth to live young.

PODOKESAURUS
"Swift-footed Lizard"

Podokesaurus (po-DOKE-ee-sawr-us) was a very small coelurosaur that lived about the same time as *Coelophysis*. *Podokesaurus* was about 3 feet (90 cm) long and probably a little more than 15 inches (38 cm) tall.

Podokesaurus was closely related to *Coelophysis* and probably resembled that dinosaur. Some authorities think that they may be the same. Like *Coelophysis, Podokesaurus* was fleet-footed. Some of the many footprints found in the Triassic rock of the Connecticut River Valley may have been made by this little dinosaur.

Podokesaurus fossil bones have been found in Massachusetts. Fragments found in western Texas indicate that similar coelurosaurs lived there during the same time period. One of these is named *Spinosuchus* (spy-no-SOOK-us).

Podokesaurus

SEGISAURUS
"Segi Lizard"

Segisaurus (SEE-gih-sawr-us), whose name refers to the canyon in Arizona where it was found, was a rabbit-sized coelurosaur that lived in Arizona during the last stages of the Triassic period and perhaps during the early part of the Jurassic. It was a speedy animal, and this was its best protection against predators. *Segisaurus* was different from other coelurosaurs. It had a collarbone, and its leg bones were solid instead of hollow.

Segisaurus

Prosauropods
"Sauropod Ancestors"

Prosauropods (pro-SAWR-o-pods) were another class of saurischian dinosaurs. They lived in North America during the last half of the Triassic.

Prosauropods, as the name suggests, may have been the ancestors of the **sauropods**—large, four-legged, brontosaur-like dinosaurs. The prosauropods found in North America were rather small. However, large kinds have

13

been found in other parts of the world, and at least one of them may have lived here.

Unlike coelurosaurs, prosauropods had heavy bones. Their skulls were small. Their teeth were not pointed like those of the meat-eating coelurosaurs, but leaf-shaped, indicating that they ate mostly plant food.

Prosauropods probably walked on all fours most of the time.

Two kinds of prosauropods are known to have lived in North America —*Anchisaurus* and *Ammosaurus*. Two others are also believed to have lived here. Isolated teeth thought by some paleontologists to be those of *Plateosaurus* and *Thecodontosaurus* have been found on our continent. These two prosauropods were common in other parts of the world and probably roamed North America also.

ANCHISAURUS
"Near Lizard"

Anchisaurus (ANG-kih-sawr-us) is also called *Yaleosaurus* (YALE-ee-o-sawr-us), "Yale (University's) Lizard." It has two names because two different people found its bones in different places. Each gave a name to the dinosaur he found. Later it was decided the two were the same kind of dinosaur. Scientists prefer to use the name *Anchisaurus,* which was given first. However, in the United States *Yaleosaurus* is often used.

Anchisaurus was one of the earliest North American prosauropods. It was not a large creature, but it was one of the largest dinosaurs of North America in its lifetime. From the tip of the small head to the end of its long tail, this dinosaur measured about 8 feet (2.5 m).

Anchisaurus's neck and heavy tail were each nearly as long as its bulky body. The short, heavy legs had short, narrow feet with four toes. Sometimes *Anchisaurus* walked on all fours, but when in a hurry it probably ran on its stocky hind legs, which were longer than the front legs. *Anchisaurus* must have been in a hurry often. Phytosaurs and *Coelophysis* shared its environment. Some phytosaurs had heads 4 feet (1.2 m) long. They probably had *Anchisaurus* for dinner sometimes.

Anchisaurus had blunt teeth, which indicates that it ate mostly plants.

Anchisaurus

There is evidence that these animals may have browsed in herds for protection.

Anchisaurus probably ranged all across the North American continent during the last half of the Triassic. *Anchisaurus* bones and footprints have been found in the Connecticut Valley and in the Southwest.

AMMOSAURUS
"Sand Lizard"

Ammosaurus (AM-o-sawr-us) was a neighbor of *Anchisaurus* and *Coelophysis* in Connecticut during the Late Triassic period, some 200 million years ago. This prosauropod was 7 feet (about 2 m) long.

Ammosaurus was very similar to *Anchisaurus,* except that it had broad feet and a slightly larger head. Like *Anchisaurus, Ammosaurus* had shorter front legs than hind legs. Sometimes this dinosaur walked on all fours and sometimes on two legs. The skull was small and the teeth were flat or peglike. *Ammosaurus* probably ate plants. This prosauropod had evolved a little closer to sauropods.

Ammosaurus remains have also been found in Arizona along with huge crocodilian reptiles and *Segisaurus.*

Ammosaurus

PLATEOSAURUS
"Flat Lizard"

Plateosaurus (PLAY-tee-uh-sawr-us) may have lived in North America. A tooth found in Nova Scotia looks somewhat like those of a *Plateosaurus* found in Germany. If it is finally proven that these dinosaurs did live here, then they were the giants among North American Triassic dinosaurs.

The German *Plateosaurus* was about 20 feet (6 m) long and perhaps weighed as much as a rhinoceros. This prosauropod had a rather small head, a long neck, and a long tail. The tail was almost half the length of the very bulky body. The broad, flat teeth of this dinosaur, from which it got its name, indicate that it was a plant eater. The hind legs were long and powerful, with broad feet, long toes, and strong claws. Though short, the forelegs were strong. *Plateosaurus* may occasionally have reared up to reach higher plant leaves, but probably spent most of its life on all fours. The hands were strong enough to help support part of the weight of the body.

This prosauropod has been found on most of the other continents of the world.

Plateosaurus

17

Thecodontosaurus

phytosaur

Thecodontosaurus *would have made a good meal for this crocodile-like reptile, the phytosaur.*

THECODONTOSAURUS
"Socket-toothed Lizard"

Thecodontosaurus (thee-kuh-DON-tuh-sawr-us) was the earliest prosauropod we know about. It had not evolved far from the thecodonts. This ancestor of *Brontosaurus* may have appeared in North America about the middle of the Triassic and lived to the end of the period.

Although *Thecodontosaurus* was not a large dinosaur, it may have been one of the largest North American Triassic dinosaurs. Only *Plateosaurus* would have been larger. From the tip of the short snout to the end of the very long tail, *Thecodontosaurus* measured about 10 feet (3 m). The body was bulky, but most of the length was made up by the long neck and tail. The arms and legs were slender and equipped with four long fingers and toes. The forelimbs were shorter than the hind legs, but like its close relative *Anchisaurus, Thecodontosaurus* walked on all fours. It may have stood on its hind legs when reaching for food or when running.

The worst enemy of *Thecodontosaurus* was probably the phytosaur. *Thecodontosaurus* would have made a good meal for such a creature.

Thecodontosaurus probably ate plants, small lizards, and rat-sized mammals. Its front teeth were serrated, but its head was too small for it to have eaten large animals. Its back teeth were peglike, and like *Anchisaurus,* it probably browsed on low leaves and shrubs.

This successful dinosaur has been found all over the world. Some scientists believe that it lived in North America also. They have found teeth which they think belong to this dinosaur. Other paleontologists think the teeth may have belonged to another kind of dinosaur, an ornithischian.

Carnosaurs
"Meat-eating Lizards"

Large theropods are called carnosaurs (KARN-uh-sawrs). Although several Triassic carnosaurs have been found in other parts of the world, fossil bones of only one North American Triassic carnosaur have been found so far. An incomplete skeleton of a dinosaur named *Poposaurus* (POPE-uh-sawr-us) was found in Wyoming. Although little is known about *Poposaurus,* it is important because finding its few bones tells us that large theropods did live here during the Triassic period.

There are clues that suggest that carnosaurs lived in other parts of North America. A carnosaur tooth was found in North Carolina, and many tracks left in Triassic mud along the Connecticut River Valley in Massachusetts are thought to have been made by carnosaurs. One carnosaur has been named *Gigandipus* (jih-GAN-dih-pus). Another, which left tracks in Dinosaur State Park in Connecticut, is called *Eubrontes* (you-BRON-teez).

Besides establishing that carnosaurs lived here during the Triassic period, the *Eubrontes* tracks are important for another reason. Some of them are thought to have been made while the animal was swimming. They are the first evidence that at least some of the large meat-eating dinosaurs could swim.

All carnosaurs were flesh eaters. They had short necks and huge heads filled with formidable teeth. Their bones were solid, to carry their heavy weight, and they walked on two birdlike hind feet. Long tails counterbalanced their short bodies and heavy heads. Their front legs were very short and armed with talons. Carnosaurs lived in every period of the Mesozoic.

Gigandipus may have been a species of the European carnosaur *Teratosaurus* (teh-RAT-uh-sawr-us), which lived during the same period. It was about 20 feet (6 m) long and weighed one-half ton (450 kg).

Eubrontes is thought to resemble a 20-foot (6-m) carnosaur, *Dilophosaurus* (die-LO-fuh-sawr-us), which lived during the final stages of the Triassic and the early part of the Jurassic.

3

The Jurassic,
a Period of Giants

As the Triassic period came to an end about 190 million years ago, the giant amphibians and phytosaurs of that period died out. Dinosaurs took their place as rulers of the earth during the Jurassic.

The Jurassic period lasted some 55 million years. Many changes took place during that time. The great supercontinent began breaking up. However, the northern section (including North America, Europe, and Asia) remained fastened together and is called Laurasia. Some parts of the continent sank. Mountains pushed up in other parts. Great shallow seas and lakes covered most of western North America until late into the period. The Gulf and West Coast states were under water.

In very early Jurassic times, the Southwest and much of the region that is now Colorado, Wyoming, Idaho, and Utah were deserts that lay close to sea level. Great sand dunes drifted across the land. As the earth's crust sank, these dunes were covered by water. A long arm of sea stretched from the Arctic through what is now the Rocky Mountain region of Canada, Montana, Wyoming, and Utah. On the western side of the sea, a sliver of land formed by the emerging Rocky Mountains ran north and south from Montana to New Mexico. On the eastern side were vast lowlands broken only by low mountains in the Ozark, Ouachita, and Arbuckle mountain areas of today.

Millions of years later, in Late Jurassic times, the sunken areas rose again. Vast flat floodplains like those of the Amazon River Basin of today extended from Mexico to Canada and from central Utah to the Mississippi River. It was a lowland of dense jungles, swamps, and glades. Great wide, meandering rivers, wider than any river of today, crossed the area. These sluggish streams carried sand and silt from the mountains in the west and deposited it in layers three miles deep in some places. Far to the west there were many active volcanoes. Large parts of the Southwest were still deserts. The Gulf of Mexico covered much of Texas, Louisiana, Alabama, Mississippi, and Florida, and spread as far north as Oklahoma and Arkansas.

Little is known about the eastern half of the continent during Jurassic times. It still lay deep in the interior of the Laurasian supercontinent. Rift valleys ran between rugged granite mountains, and during most of the period the area was undergoing more or less continuous erosion. Today most of it has eroded below its level during the Mesozoic Era.

The climate of North America was hot and seasonably arid in many parts. At the beginning of the Jurassic period there was a brief drop in temperature worldwide, but it was soon followed by a long period of hot, humid, tropical or semitropical climate for most of the North American continent. Thunderstorms pelted the landscape almost daily during the wet seasons. The Jurassic was a perfect time for growing giants. Even plants became gigantic. Sequoias, ponderosa pines, and giant ferns appeared during this time, as did the world's largest land animals. Woody shrubs began to flourish during the last part of the period.

It was during the latter half of the Jurassic that dinosaurs really became dominant, and some grew to be enormous. They shared their world with a variety of creatures that are familiar today. Over a thousand kinds of insects existed. Among them were flies, ants, bees, wasps, mosquitoes, crickets, grasshoppers, moths, beetles, and termites. Frogs, salamanders, snails, turtles, and lizards were abundant. Birds, the batlike pterosaurs (TAIR-uh-sawrs) (the first flying reptiles), and very primitive mammals no larger than a cat, and more often the size of a mouse, lived alongside the giants.

Few dinosaur remains have been found in North America for the first half of the Jurassic period. However, fossils of Early Jurassic sea life are abundant. Most of the West was under water during that time. Small sharks inhabited freshwater lakes. There were plesiosaurs (PLEEZ-ee-uh-sawrs)— 50-foot (15-m) paddle-legged sea-going reptiles—and ichthyosaurs (IK-thee-uh-sawrs)—similar, dolphin-shaped marine reptiles—swimming in the seas covering what is now western North America.

Few Mesozoic fossils of any kind are found in the central or eastern part of North America, because the rocks there have eroded down to the Paleozoic level—the geological period before the Mesozoic. Fossils in Paleozoic layers are much older than dinosaurs.

Jurassic Dinosaurs

Only three dinosaurs from the Early Jurassic have been found in North America. All were theropods and all were found in Arizona. However, many kinds of dinosaurs from that period have been found in other parts of the world. And since the continents were still connected, those dinosaurs probably lived here also. The numbers of large, new, and more advanced kinds found in Late Jurassic rock tell us not only that many dinosaurs were present in the Early Jurassic but that they were rapidly evolving.

Although there are few exposed areas of Early Jurassic rock in North America, there are large areas of exposed Late Jurassic rock. Paleontologists have found at least seventeen different kinds of dinosaurs in them. Among them are the enormous four-legged plant eaters called sauropods. These were the dominant animals of the period.

This was the age of giants. Small coelurosaurs still scurried about in the underbrush, but most Jurassic theropods were large carnosaurs with huge heads and massive bodies and legs. However, it was in the Late Jurassic rock deposits that the first bird-hipped dinosaurs, or **ornithischians** (or-nih-THISS-kee-ans), in North America also were found.

DILOPHOSAURUS
"Two-crested Lizard"

Dilophosaurus (die-LO-fuh-sawr-us), a medium-sized theropod, was a preview of bigger carnosaurs to come. This strange theropod roamed the plains of what is now Arizona sometime during the last days of the Triassic or the beginning of the Jurassic. It measured 20 feet (6 m) from the tip of the snout to the tip of the tail.

Like its ancestor *Coelophysis, Dilophosaurus* was built for speed and walked or ran on powerful hind legs. It had solid bones like all carnosaurs, and the feet were birdlike and four-toed. However, only three toes left tracks in the mud, because the fourth toe was very short.

23

Dilophosaurus

The front legs, or arms, were short—about half the length of the hind legs. Each had three long, clawed fingers that could be used for grasping.

Dilophosaurus had a large skull, but unlike the skulls of most carnosaurs, it was very delicate. Two great crests ran lengthwise across the top of the head. No one knows the purpose of these crests.

The daggerlike teeth were perfect for eating meat, but *Dilophosaurus* probably used its powerful hind feet and eagle-like claws to kill its prey. The jaws were too weak for this task.

Dilophosaurus appears to have been a desert dweller. Its fossils have been found in Arizona, which was a desert during Early Jurassic times.

Because of the size of this meat eater, it probably had no enemies. The only other dinosaurs known from the Early Jurassic in North America are the tiny *Segisaurus,* which lived in the same area of Arizona that *Dilophosaurus* roamed, and a still larger crested theropod not yet named, which has recently been found in the same area. *Dilophosaurus* was originally mistaken for *Megalosaurus,* but no *Megalosaurus* has been discovered in North America.

ORNITHOLESTES "Bird Robber" and *COELURUS* "Hollow Bones"

Ornitholestes (or-nith-o-LESS-teez) and *Coelurus* (see-LURE-us) are the only small coelurosaurs that have been found from the latter half of the Jurassic period. Some scientists consider them to be the same, but others do not agree. They think that though *Ornitholestes* and *Coelurus* were quite similar in some respects, they were different in others.

These animals lived along the forested seashore. Both were lightly built and, like all coelurosaurs, had hollow bones. They closely resembled their ancestor *Coelophysis,* but were slightly smaller. *Ornitholestes* measured about 6 feet (1.8 m) from the tip of the tiny head to the end of the 3-foot (90-cm)

Ornith

tail. *Coelurus* was about the same size. They both had short, flexible necks, and their jaws were filled with curved, razor-sharp teeth.

Like *Coelophysis,* they walked on two long, slender, birdlike legs. Built for speed, they probably were the most agile animals of their time. The long tails were held out behind to act as a counterbalance as they fled from danger or chased lizards, young dinosaurs, large insects, and other small animals.

Although *Ornitholestes*'s name means "bird robber," this coelurosaur probably ate any small animal it could find. Perhaps it even scavenged on carcasses left by larger predators. *Ornitholestes* may have eaten reptile eggs, too.

These animals had short arms with three long fingers. *Ornitholestes* might have been able to use one finger like a thumb, so it could catch and hold prey with its sharp claws. It is not known for sure whether *Coelurus* could do this.

Ornitholestes and *Coelurus* must have been good hunters. Although their heads were only 6 inches (15 cm) long, their eye, nostril, and ear cavities were very large. This indicates that they had very good senses of sight, smell, and hearing. They needed them. Along with speed, these were their only protection. This must have been sufficient, as *Coelurus* may have lived on into Early Cretaceous times.

Fossils of these two dinosaurs have been found along with the giant carnosaurs *Allosaurus* and *Ceratosaurus* in the Rocky Mountain area of North America.

ALLOSAURUS
"Other" or "Different" Lizard

Allosaurus (AL-uh-sawr-us) is also called *Antrodemus* (an-tro-DEE-mus), meaning "cavern-boned." It was a truly fearsome animal. This giant carnosaur, which lived during the last half of the Jurassic period, had heavy bones and powerful muscles. The average *Allosaurus* measured 35 feet (10.5 m) from the tip of the nose to the end of the tail and weighed between 3 and 4 tons (2.7 and 3.6 metric tons). When it stood erect, the top of the head was 15 feet (4.5 m) above the ground. In a running stance with the

Allosaurus (Antrodemu

heavy tail stretched out behind, the hips were 8 feet (2.5 m) above the ground. The largest *Allosaurus* found to date measured 45 feet (13.5 m) long and stood 16.5 feet (5 m) tall!

Like all theropods, this flesh eater walked on two legs. Its strong hind legs were built for speed. It is believed that *Allosaurus* could run at least as fast as a man. The birdlike feet had three toes plus a dewclaw. Their imprint in 6-foot (1.8-m) strides has been found in Jurassic mud. Some scientists think that *Allosaurus* and all other theropods may have been warm-blooded.

The strong front legs were only half as long as the hind legs. The three fingers on each hand were also strong and, like the toes, armed with sharp claws.

Allosaurus's enormous 3-foot (90-cm) head was supported by a short, strong neck. Its eyes were very large, twice the size of any other carnosaur's eyes. They were shaded by low, arrowhead-shaped crests at the brow. The skin probably was tough and leathery.

This formidable animal had an enormous mouth which was filled with 2–4-inch (5–10-cm) saberlike teeth that were serrated on both edges. They could cut, saw, or tear. A new tooth grew in as soon as an old one fell out. The jaws were hinged something like a snake's so that this carnosaur could swallow huge chunks of flesh or small animals whole.

Allosaurus probably ate all kinds of meat. We know it ate *Apatosaurus* because scientists have found *Apatosaurus* vertebrae that had *Allosaurus* tooth marks on them. It is not known whether *Allosaurus* killed the *Apatosaurus* or ate an animal that was already dead. *Allosaurus* may have hunted in groups or pairs. A pair could have killed such a large animal easily. However, tracks found in Texas tell the story of a single *Allosaurus* stalking a large sauropod. A fully grown *Allosaurus* probably had no enemies.

Allosaurus was an intelligent animal and probably lived in family groups. Adult and juvenile bones have been found together in central Utah. The smallest juvenile was 10 feet (3 m) long and 3½ feet (1 m) tall.

A newly hatched baby may have been no larger than 20 inches (50 cm) long. It must have required a great deal of care and protection in a world of giants. It would have been impossible for such a small baby to keep up with the adults. Some scientists think dinosaurs may have had "nurseries" with one or more adults caring for all the young of the herd. Giraffes care for their young in this manner.

Allosaurus roamed a wide area of the North American jungles in the region that is now the Rocky Mountains. Fossils of this carnosaur have been found in many western states and Canada.

Allosaurus died out soon after the end of the Jurassic period, but other carnosaurs evolved to take its place. *Creosaurus* (KREE-o-sawr-us) and *Labrosaurus* (LAB-ro-sawr-us) are names given to fossil remains which later proved to be juvenile *Allosaurus*.

Allosaurus shared the swamps and plains with many other Jurassic giants, both carnosaurs and sauropods. One of these giants was a meat-eating dinosaur called *Torvosaurus* (TOR-vuh-sawr-us), "savage lizard." A 12-inch (30-cm) claw, several enormous teeth, and other bones belonging to this gigantic meat eater have recently been found in Colorado. This dinosaur was more advanced than *Allosaurus*. It was totally different from any other carnosaur yet discovered. Although *Torvosaurus* was larger than *Allosaurus*, its skull was shorter. The forearms were very short and the body was massive.

CERATOSAURUS
"Horned Lizard"

Ceratosaurus (sair-AT-o-sawr-us), another large Jurassic carnosaur, shared the jungles of North America with *Allosaurus*. About 15–20 feet (4.5–6 m) long, *Ceratosaurus* looked very like its cousin *Allosaurus*, except this dinosaur had a bladelike horn on its nose. *Ceratosaurus* is the only known meat eater to have a horn. It also had bony knobs above each eye.

Like *Allosaurus*, *Ceratosaurus* had a huge head and saberlike teeth. The head was balanced by a long, thick tail. Like all theropods, the "horned lizard" walked on two legs. It had three-toed, birdlike feet. The front legs were short, but unlike *Allosaurus*, *Ceratosaurus* had four fingers. The two outer digits were much shorter than the two center ones.

Ceratosaurus was a powerful, savage hunter and probably caught and ate baby *Stegosaurus* and other small dinosaurs.

Ceratosaurus fossils have been found in the same areas of North America where *Allosaurus* lived. However, this unusual dinosaur is found much less often than *Allosaurus*.

Ceratosaurus

Other carnosaurs lived during this period. A few bones of two new kinds have recently been found in Utah.

Marshosaurus (MARSH-uh-sawr-us), a neighbor of *Allosaurus* and *Ceratosaurus,* was a medium-sized theropod. It is estimated that this dinosaur was about 6 feet (1.8 m) tall, 17 feet (5 m) long, and weighed about one-half ton (450 kg).

This carnosaur had a large head. The mouth was filled with long, narrow, serrated teeth that were flattened and sharply curved. Like all carnosaurs, this dinosaur walked on two legs.

Although *Marshosaurus* had some features similar to those of a coelurosaur, in general it must have looked rather like a small version of *Allosaurus* as it roamed the jungles of western North America, seeking smaller animals for dinner.

The bulldog-faced *Stokesosaurus* (STOKES-uh-sawr-us) was a still smaller Jurassic carnosaur. From the few bones known for this dinosaur, it is estimated that an adult was about 13 feet (4 m) long and 5 feet (1.5 m) tall. *Stokesosaurus* had a shorter snout than *Allosaurus* and was a more advanced carnosaur. *Stokesosaurus* probably was more closely related to *Tyrannosaurus* than to other Jurassic meat eaters.

Like all meat-eating dinosaurs, *Stokesosaurus* walked on two legs and had long, serrated teeth. It fed on small reptiles and mammals that roamed western North America during the Late Jurassic age.

Both *Marshosaurus* and *Stokesaurus* have been found with fossils of *Allosaurus.*

Sauropods
"Lizard-footed"

By the middle of the Jurassic period, sauropods (SAWR-uh-pods) had replaced prosauropods in North America and were the most common land animals. Although they were plentiful in other parts of the world before that, no earlier ones have been found in North America.

Sauropods were gigantic plant-eating animals with very long necks, and heads that were small in comparison with their bodies. Many had long, whiplike tails which may have been used for defense. Some scientists think that sauropods carried their tails stretched out behind. Others believe that the tails were dragged along the ground.

Sauropod feet and legs were broad and elephant-like. In order to carry their great weight, these peaceful animals walked on all four legs. Their feet and leg bones were solid and massive, but the vertebrae were filled with holes to make the animal lighter.

Why did the sauropods grow so big? No one knows. It may be because they had large pituitary glands. It has been suggested that they grew so large because the solar radiation was greater then. Some scientists think that sauropods never stopped growing and that they may have lived to be a hundred years old or more. Other scientists suggest that the great size of sauropods was an adaptation for heat control. Their huge bodies may have acted as heat reservoirs that cooled very slowly, making it unnecessary for the animals to eat enormous amounts of food to maintain a relatively even body temperature.

It was once thought that all sauropods lived in swamps or lakes because they were too big and heavy to live on land. Many scientists now believe that sauropods were land dwellers and only occasionally swam in rivers and lakes, as elephants do today.

Sauropods probably browsed on twigs and needles of tall pines, firs, and sequoia trees. Evidence of this has been found in a fossilized sauropod stomach. Broken bits of bone were also found in the stomach. This may mean that sauropods ate some meat also, but scientists consider this unlikely. Since sauropods had no molars, or grinding teeth, for chewing coarse material, they may have swallowed small rounded pebbles called gastroliths or "gizzard stones" to grind the food, as some birds do today. Gizzard stones have been found with some sauropod remains.

Sauropods were slow and are often considered unintelligent because their brains were rather small for their size. However, their brains were at least as big as a dog's, and perhaps that was as large as they needed to be to meet the sauropods' needs. Sauropods were quite successful animals and lived to the end of the Mesozoic age.

Fossilized tracks found in Texas indicate that sauropods sometimes moved in herds, and traveled about the forests and river plains with their young protected by a ring of adult animals much as elephants do. This has led some scientists to believe that sauropods were not as unintelligent as was

33

once thought. A newly hatched baby sauropod was probably no larger than a house cat.

It has been suggested that young sauropods may have been born alive. However, few paleontologists believe this, because dinosaur eggs have been found in France that are thought to have been laid by a small sauropod, *Hypselosaurus* (HIP-see-lo-sawr-us). These eggs are nearly round, with a long diameter of 10 inches (25 cm)—two times the size of an ostrich egg. They have a rough, sandpaperlike surface covered with small bumps, and were laid in sand nests. As many as five have been found in one clutch.

Fossilized skin impressions show that sauropods had coarse, granular scales like some lizards of today.

At least six different kinds of sauropods are known to have lived in North America during the Late Jurassic period. These are *Apatosaurus (Brontosaurus), Camarasaurus, Haplocanthosaurus, Diplodocus, Barosaurus,* and *Brachiosaurus.*

APATOSAURUS
"Deceptive Lizard"

This giant sauropod is better known as *Brontosaurus* (BRON-tuh-sawr-us), meaning "thunder lizard." However, *Apatosaurus* (ah-PAT-uh-sawr-us) is the correct name because that was the first name given to this animal.

Like all sauropods, *Apatosaurus* walked on all four legs. The front legs were shorter than the hind legs, and the shoulders were lower than the hips. This gave the back a beautiful arch.

The average *Apatosaurus* was about 75 feet (23 m) long, 15 feet (4.5 m) tall at the hips, and weighed 30 to 40 tons (27 to 36 metric tons). That is twelve times as much as a large elephant weighs! This animal would have been even heavier if the vertebrae had not developed large holes to make them lighter. The body and tail were massive. The 30-foot (9-m) tail ended in a whiplash tip.

Apatosaurus had a 20-foot (6-m) flexible neck that permitted it to browse on tall trees as giraffes do today. *Apatosaurus* nipped off leaves with peglike front teeth and swallowed them whole because it had no molars for grinding food.

The head of *Apatosaurus* was small compared to the rest of the body, but even so, it was larger than a horse's head. The mouth was about the same size as the mouth of a rhinoceros. Scientists once thought *Apatosaurus* had a short, blunt snout similar to that of *Camarasaurus*. This is now known to be incorrect. The snout was long, and the head more closely resembled that of *Diplodocus*.

Apatosaurus probably had excellent hearing and good senses of sight and smell. The eyes were large. The nostrils were placed high on the head, directly in front of the eyes, and were slightly raised. *Apatosaurus* was a slow-moving animal. It could probably travel no faster than two to four miles, or three to six kilometers, per hour.

The feet and legs of *Apatosaurus* were thick and pillarlike, similar to an elephant's. Its broad, round, padded feet left footprints nearly 1 yard (90 cm) long and 26 inches (65 cm) wide. Each forefoot had one long inner claw. Each hind foot had three claws.

Apatosaurus was like an elephant in other ways too. This plains and forest dweller probably traveled in herds with larger members on the outside of the herd and younger or weaker members in the center. This helped protect them from their worst enemy, *Allosaurus*.

Apatosaurus was also protected by its size and tough, thick, leathery skin. The tail, too, could have been used to lash out at enemies.

Traveling in herds and protecting the young are considered to be fairly advanced behavior. Some scientists think *Apatosaurus* may not have been such a stupid animal as has been supposed. Although its brain was small, about the size of an adult human's fist, brain size alone is not a true measure of mental ability.

Apatosaurus fossils have been found with those of *Allosaurus, Ceratosaurus, Marshosaurus, Stokesosaurus,* and many other kinds of sauropods of the Late Jurassic period. This sauropod roamed a wide area of the western part of North America, from Montana to Baja California. Other plant eaters also lived in the same area.

Atlantosaurus (at-LAN-tuh-sawr-us) and *Titanosaurus* (tie-TAN-uh-sawr-us) are other names that have been given to this gigantic sauropod.

Apatosaurus (Brontosaurus)

CAMARASAURUS
"Chambered Lizard"

Camarasaurus (KAM-uh-ruh-sawr-us) was the most common sauropod in North America during the Middle and Late Jurassic period. This sauropod may have been one of the earliest to appear on the North American continent. It was also one of the smallest sauropods.

Camarasaurus was sturdily built like its close cousin *Apatosaurus,* but was somewhat shorter. *Camarasaurus* had a shorter neck and a much shorter, more powerful tail. An adult *Camarasaurus* measured from 30 to 60 feet (9 to 18 m) in length and reached a height of 15 feet (4.5 m) at the hips.

Camarasaurus was different from most sauropods. Its front legs were nearly as long as its hind legs. This made the line of the backbone nearly horizontal. The skull was larger, but more lightly built. Backbone cavities are the "chambers" for which it was named.

Like all sauropods, this peaceful four-legged dinosaur was a plant eater. The peglike teeth, which were 3 inches (8 cm) long, were suitable only for grazing. This sauropod probably browsed on lower vegetation than did others that lived with it.

Only its size and traveling in herds protected *Camarasaurus* from giant predators like *Allosaurus* and *Ceratosaurus. Camarasaurus* ranged throughout the western part of North America from the mid-Jurassic to the very early Cretaceous.

Fossils of many young *Camarasaurus* have been found. One was only 16 feet (about 5 m) long. *Uintasaurus* (you-IN-tuh-sawr-us) and *Morosaurus* (MOR-o-sawr-us) are names given to dinosaurs that later proved to be young *Camarasaurus.*

Remains of a very young sauropod were found in Wyoming. This dinosaur was given the name *Elosaurus* (EEL-o-sawr-us). Some scientists believe that *Elosaurus* is either a juvenile of *Camarasaurus* or one of its close relatives.

Camarasaurus

HAPLOCANTHOSAURUS
"Single-spined Lizard"

Haplocanthosaurus (hap-luh-KANTH-uh-sawr-us) was another early North American sauropod that lived in Middle Jurassic times. But it was not as common as *Camarasaurus*. *Haplocanthosaurus* was smaller than most sauropods. The largest measured 72 feet (22 m) from the tip of the nose to the end of the tail.

This enormous plant eater had a long body, but a relatively short neck and tail. The tail was less massive than that of *Camarasaurus*. This dinosaur's vertebrae were nearly solid. Its front legs were about two thirds as long as its hind legs, and it carried its backbone nearly horizontal.

Haplocanthosaurus fossil bones have been found in Colorado.

Haplocanthosaurus

DIPLODOCUS
"Double Beam"

Diplodocus (dih-PLOD-uh-kus) looked like *Apatosaurus* in some ways. It had a long neck, a long whiplash tail, and short front legs. But *Diplodocus* was much longer than *Apatosaurus* and weighed less. The neck and tail were much longer, but the body was slimmer. Its name refers to the double spines on its vertebrae.

One of the longest of all the dinosaurs, *Diplodocus* measured 90 feet (27 m) from the end of the nose to the tip of the tail and stood 13 feet (4 m) at the hips. This sleek animal weighed about 25 tons (22.5 metric tons). Most of its length was in its long, snaky neck, which measured 26 feet (8 m), and its 45-foot (13.5-m) tail.

Diplodocus must have nipped off the tenderest leaves from the tops of the trees, because the teeth were weak and peglike and were located only in the front of the mouth. The head was generally larger than those of other sauropods and had a long, slender snout. The skull measured 2 feet (60 cm) long.

Because the nostrils of *Diplodocus* were high on the head, scientists used to think that it lived on the bottom of lakes and used its long neck as a snorkel. It is now known that it would have been impossible for the animal to breathe in such deep water because of the pressure of the water. It has been suggested that having the nostrils on top of the head may have been a way of protecting the nostrils from harm while the animal ate from tree-tops. Another theory is that the high nostril position allowed *Diplodocus* to breathe while eating continuously.

Diplodocus may have been a swamp and jungle dweller. Perhaps it enjoyed frequent wading in lakes and streams just as elephants do. Like all sauropods, this dinosaur had great padded, elephantine feet. Each foot had three powerful claws.

Diplodocus couldn't travel fast enough to escape the huge carnosaurs that were its neighbors. Its tail was an effective defense weapon, but the chief defense of this sauropod was its size. *Diplodocus* also probably lived and traveled in herds, and their long necks would have helped the herd members watch for an enemy's approach.

Diplodocus existed on into the Early Cretaceous period. Its remains have

Diplodocus

been found in the Rocky Mountain areas of North America. Near neighbors were other sauropods, large carnosaurs, *Stegosaurus,* and *Camptosaurus.*

One of the first sauropods ever discovered was given the name *Amphi-coelias* (am-fih-SEE-lee-us). *Amphicoelias* is now believed to be the same animal as *Diplodocus.*

BAROSAURUS
"Heavy Lizard"

Barosaurus (BAR-uh-sawr-us) was like *Diplodocus* in some ways. It was about the same length, 90 feet (27 m), and the legs were very similar. But *Barosaurus* had a much longer neck. Its neck was about 30 feet (9 m) long! Some of the vertebrae were 3 feet (90 cm) long. This giraffe-like animal used its extraordinarily long neck to browse on treetops that other dinosaurs could not reach.

The body was massive like that of *Apatosaurus,* but the tail was relatively short. *Barosaurus* probably swallowed stones to help grind the plant food it ate. Seven highly polished gastroliths, or gizzard stones, were found with fossils of one specimen.

Barosaurus roamed the jungles of South Dakota and Colorado during the last half of the Jurassic, along with other sauropods, the giant carnosaurs, and *Stegosaurus.*

Barosaurus

BRACHIOSAURUS
"Arm Lizard"

Brachiosaurus (BRAK-ee-uh-sawr-us) was an enormous sauropod, perhaps the largest land animal that ever lived. This giant dinosaur lived in the western part of North America between 165 and 100 million years ago.

The average *Brachiosaurus* measured 75–80 feet (23–24 m) in length and 40 feet (12 m) from the top of the head to the bottom of the feet. That is taller than a four-story building! It has been suggested that this animal might have weighed 75 or 80 tons (67.5 or 72 metric tons)—twelve times as much as a large African elephant. The body was almost twice as massive as that of *Apatosaurus.*

Like all sauropods, *Brachiosaurus* had pillarlike legs and broad feet. But the front legs of this dinosaur were much larger and longer than the forelegs of other sauropods. They were even longer than the hind legs; that is why it is called the "arm lizard." *Brachiosaurus*'s shoulders were 19 feet (5.5 m) above the ground, and its back sloped, giraffe fashion, from the shoulders to the hips.

Brachiosaurus had a short tail, but an exceptionally long neck—about 28 feet (8.5 m). *Brachiosaurus* could reach to the tops of 40-foot (12-m) trees to browse. The head was small for the size of the body, and the jaws were weak. However, the stomach was large. *Brachiosaurus* must have had to eat large quantities of leaves continuously to stay alive.

Brachiosaurus's nostrils were placed atop a narrow raised crest above the eyes. The neck and back bones were very light, but strong, while the bones of the lower part of the body were massive. It was once thought that *Brachiosaurus* lived in water 35–40 feet (10.5–12 m) deep, with just the nostrils sticking out. We now know it would have been impossible for the animal to breathe at such depths. It is probable that *Brachiosaurus* did often wade in lakes and eat water plants, but it did not live completely submerged in water.

Brachiosaurus was a slow animal. It is estimated that it traveled about two miles (three kilometers) per hour. Only its great size and tough, leathery hide protected it from *Allosaurus* and *Ceratosaurus.* Some scientists think that a *Brachiosaurus* that was successful in avoiding enemies could have lived to be two hundred years old.

Brachiosaurus

Brachiosaurus fossils have been found in the Rocky Mountain area. This sauropod lived with *Barosaurus, Apatosaurus, Stegosaurus,* and the huge carnosaurs. *Brachiosaurus* was a very successful dinosaur. It didn't become extinct until Early Cretaceous times.

"SUPERSAURUS" and "ULTRASAURUS"

Bones of two sauropods that may have been even larger than *Brachiosaurus* have been found in Colorado. The skeletons are incomplete, but it is believed that these animals were closely related to *Brachiosaurus* and resembled it, which means that their front legs were probably longer than their hind legs.

Although not enough bones have been found for us to know exactly how these animals looked, we can be sure that they were truly gigantic. These peaceful plant eaters may have been the largest land animals that ever lived. These dinosaurs haven't yet received official scientific names. The nicknames are from their gigantic proportions.

It is estimated that "Supersaurus" measured 90–100 feet (27–30 m) from the tip of the nose to the end of the tail. It may have stood more than 50 feet (15 m) tall and must have weighed 80 tons (72 metric tons) or more. That is fifteen times as heavy as a large African elephant! The shoulder blades were 8 feet (2.5 m) long and the hipbones were 6½ feet (2 m) wide. *Brachiosaurus*'s hipbones were only 4 feet (1.2 m) wide.

"Ultrasaurus" must have been even larger. It may have been more than 100 feet (30 m) long and perhaps 50–60 feet (15–18 m) tall. This sauropod could have looked over a five-story building! Its shoulder blade, the largest dinosaur bone ever found, is nearly 9 feet (2.75 m) long. The legs may have been 20 feet (6 m) long, which is as long as a giraffe is tall. If "Ultrasaurus" was built like *Brachiosaurus,* it weighed well over 80 tons (72 metric tons).

These enormous animals, like all sauropods, walked on four pillarlike legs. From the size of the neck vertebrae that have been found, it is estimated that their necks may have been as much as 40 feet (12 m) long. The smallest vertebra is 3 feet (90 cm) long; the largest is 5 feet (1.5 m) long.

These huge creatures lived about 140 million years ago, during the same time as *Allosaurus, Ceratosaurus,* and other giant carnosaurs. No one knows why they grew so big. Perhaps it was for protection. Perhaps it was because they just kept growing as long as they lived. Perhaps "Supersaurus" and "Ultrasaurus" lived even longer than two hundred years.

They probably browsed on the tops of the very tallest trees. They must have had to eat continuously all day long. Scientists doubt that such huge animals could have been truly warm-blooded. If they had been, they would have had to eat several times as much as a large elephant! Some scientists believe that the huge bodies of these animals acted as heat reservoirs, so that they did not need to eat enough to generate heat for their bodies.

Ornithischians "Bird-hipped"

Saurischians, the lizard-hipped dinosaurs, were the dominant animals of the Jurassic, but there were a few ornithischians, too. The earliest bird-hipped dinosaurs found in North America lived during the Middle Jurassic period. Ornithischians lived on other continents as early as the Late Triassic, and some may have lived in North America at that time. Although no bones have yet been found, dinosaur footprints found in the Connecticut Valley in eastern United States and in Glen Canyon in southwestern United States provide good evidence that ornithischians lived there in late Triassic or early Jurassic times.

The animals that made the tracks walked on all fours at least part of the time. Both front and hind feet left tracks in the mud. The tracks, named *Anomoepus* (an-o-MEE-pus), show no claw marks and have five fingers on the hands and three toes on the feet. These are the clues that make scientists believe the tracks made by ornithischian dinosaurs.

Nearly all ornithischians had blunt hoofs instead of claws on their feet, and most had five fingers and three toes. Some were two-legged and some were four-legged. Unlike the saurischian dinosaurs, all ornithischians were plant eaters and almost all had horny beaks.

There were four kinds of ornithischians: **ornithopods** (or-NITH-uh-pods), those that walked on two legs, either all the time or most of the time;

47

stegosaurs (STEG-uh-sawrs), plated dinosaurs; **ankylosaurs** (ang-KILE-uh-sawrs), armored dinosaurs; and **ceratopsians** (sair-uh-TOP-see-ans), horned dinosaurs. In North America only ornithopods and stegosaurs have been found from the Jurassic period.

Ornithopods
"Bird-footed"

Ornithopods (or-NITH-uh-pods) were the most successful of the ornithischian dinosaurs. The first we know about lived in Europe and Africa in the Late Triassic period. By the middle of the Jurassic they had spread worldwide. They survived to the end of the Cretaceous.

Except in respect to size, all ornithopod bodies were quite similar. Many evolved other special features, but like coelurosaurs, their bodies remained much the same. Most walked on two legs, although some may have dropped to all fours when eating. All had heavy, thick bodies, long tails, thick hind legs which were nearly twice as long as their front legs, and strong feet.

Four Jurassic ornithopods have been found in North America.

CAMPTOSAURUS
"Bent Lizard"

Camptosaurus (KAMP-tuh-sawr-us) was the earliest North American ornithopod we know about. This predecessor of the duckbill was very common during the Late Jurassic period. It was probably more common than any other animal except the giant sauropods.

Camptosaurus may have roamed in large herds throughout much of western North America. Like the deer of today, it lived mostly in the open areas beyond swamps and forests, browsing on low ground plants.

Many sizes of *Camptosaurus* have been found. They range from turkey

Camptosaurus

size to 17 feet (5 m) long and 7 feet (about 2 m) in height at the hips. The largest weighed around a half ton (450 kg). The smaller specimens may have been young animals.

Camptosaurus usually walked and ran on its hind legs with its body nearly horizontal. The hind legs were thick and powerful. They were built for speed, and *Camptosaurus* could probably run swiftly. Speed and herding were its best defenses against its natural enemies, the giant carnosaurs *Allosaurus* and *Ceratosaurus*. *Camptosaurus* was a successful animal and survived into the Cretaceous period.

When feeding, *Camptosaurus* probably bent down (hence its name) and walked on all fours like a kangaroo. This dinosaur may have walked on all fours more than other ornithopods. The front legs were only about half as long as the hind legs, but were strong. The five-fingered hands were broad and could help support the animal's weight.

The neck was short and the small head was long, broad, and rather flat. Instead of front teeth, *Camptosaurus* had a sharp, horny beak. The back jaws were lined with very small, chisel-shaped teeth that worked like nutcrackers to crush the tough vegetation it ate.

Camptosaurus shared the Jurassic plains with *Stegosaurus*. Sauropods roamed nearby forests.

DRYOSAURUS
"Oak Lizard"

Dryosaurus (DRY-o-sawr-us) was one of the most graceful of the ornithopods. This dinosaur was smaller and more slender than *Camptosaurus*. It is estimated that it measured 7–12 feet (2–3.5 m) from the tip of its nose to the end of the tail and weighed 150–170 pounds (68–77 kg). The largest stood about 4 feet (1.2 m) tall at the hips.

Like *Camptosaurus*, this dinosaur was bipedal (walked on two legs) and carried its body horizontally. The front legs were short and well developed, and *Dryosaurus* probably occasionally dropped down on all fours to eat ground vegetation. But unlike *Camptosaurus*, this ornithopod had very long and slender hind legs. The feet had three long, strong, forward-pointing toes. *Dryosaurus* was undoubtedly a swift-running animal.

The head of *Dryosaurus* was small and ended in a slim, beaklike snout. The teeth were shaped something like oak leaves, and that is why this ornithopod was named "oak lizard." *Dryosaurus* had cheeks like a mammal's to hold food while it chewed.

This peaceful little plant eater grazed on ground plants in open glades near woodlands of Jurassic Colorado and Wyoming. It lived from Late Jurassic to Early Cretaceous times.

Dryosaurus

OTHNIELIA

Jurassic *Othnielia* (oth-NEEL-ee-uh), named in honor of Othniel Charles Marsh, American paleontologist, was a turkey-sized ornithopod—about 2½ feet (75 cm) long. Like all ornithopods, this dinosaur walked on its hind legs, which were about twice as long as its front legs. Because this dinosaur's legs were long and slender, it was probably a swift runner. Speed was needed to escape the giant carnosaurs of the period.

Othnielia's head was small, but the eyes were fairly large. The snout was short and narrow. Unlike most ornithopods, *Othnielia* had a few teeth in the front part of the upper jaw as well as grinding teeth in the back jaws. Each hand of this little plant eater had five fingers. The fifth finger was almost at right angles to the others, instead of being parallel as were the fingers of *Dryosaurus.*

Also called *Laosaurus* (LAY-uh-sawr-us), "fossil lizard," *Othnielia* grazed alongside *Dryosaurus* and *Camptosaurus* in open glades. Its fossils have been found in Wyoming and Colorado along with those of *Ceratosaurus, Allosaurus, Ornitholestes,* and most of the huge sauropods.

Othnielia (Laosaurus)

A larger, different animal whose fossils were found in Wyoming in Late Cretaceous rock has also been called *Laosaurus.* It is very similar to the European *Hypsilophodon* and may be the same as that animal. It ranged in size from 8 to 10 feet (2.5 to 3 m) long and weighed up to 175 pounds (80 kg).

NANOSAURUS
"Dwarf Lizard"

Nanosaurus (NAN-uh-sawr-us) is one of the smallest North American dinosaurs ever found. From the few bones that are known, it is estimated that this little dinosaur was about the size of a turkey, perhaps 12 inches (30 cm) tall at the hips and a little over 2 feet (60 cm) long.

Nanosaurus

This graceful little ornithopod probably ran on long, slender hind legs with tail extended. It had long, slender feet and hollow bones. The body had a typical ornithopod structure, with a small head and short front legs. The jaws were lined with a single row of tiny leaf-shaped teeth.

Nanosaurus lived in Colorado and Wyoming. Its bones have been found with those of *Brachiosaurus.* Imagine how agile this little plant eater needed to be just to keep from being stepped on!

STEGOSAURUS
"Plated Lizard"

Stegosaurus (STEG-uh-sawr-us) is the only plated ornithischian found in North America. This strange-looking dinosaur appeared during the last of the Jurassic period. A close relative, *Scelidosaurus* (skel-EE-doe-sawr-us), lived in Europe in Early Jurassic days, but so far has never been found here.

Unlike the ornithopods, *Stegosaurus* walked on all four legs. This peaceful plant eater may have roamed the highlands of western North America in small herds, grazing on low ground plants such as ferns and horsetails.

The body of an average adult *Stegosaurus* was about the size of an elephant. It stood 11 feet (3.3 m) at the hips, was 25 feet (7.5 m) long from the tip of the nose to the end of the tail, and weighed 2–3 tons (1.8–2.7 metric tons). But the brain of *Stegosaurus* was no larger than a golf ball!

Stegosaurus's head was ridiculously small, only 16 inches (40 cm) long. It was quite narrow and ended in a rounded, turtle-like beak. The thick hind legs were long and strong. But the front legs were very short, giving the body a high arch at the hips. The front feet had five toes and the hind feet had four. Each toe had a hooflike claw.

Two rows of thin bony plates ran along the neck, back, and part of the tail. The tallest plates, which were over the hips, were about 2 feet (60 cm) tall. No one knows the purpose of these plates. They might have been to make the animal look larger or to attract a mate. Some scientists believe they regulated the body temperature. The plates were equipped with a network of blood vessels and were arranged alternately. Wind could flow more easily around them in this arrangement than if they had been arranged in pairs.

Such wind flow would effectively have cooled the blood as it flowed through the plates.

The tail of *Stegosaurus* was thick and heavy. The end was armed with four spikes, each a foot (30 cm) long. These may have been weapons of defense against big carnosaurs such as *Allosaurus.* For more protection, the body may have been enclosed in a heavy coat of leathery armor.

Baby *Stegosaurus* may not have had plates. Scientists have found two dog-sized babies in Dinosaur National Monument in Utah. These did not have plates. Perhaps *Stegosaurus* didn't grow plates until it was adult. Maybe only males grew them, or perhaps the babies' plates were lost by erosion through the centuries. No one really knows.

Stegosaurus probably hatched from eggs. Large oval eggs that are believed to be stegosaur eggs were found in Portugal.

Stegosaurus lived to the end of the Jurassic period. By the Early Cretaceous, all stegosaurs were extinct. Stegosaurs were the only ornithischian type that became extinct before the end of the Cretaceous period. Perhaps they were unable to adapt to the changing world. However, they did live 50 million years, and that is a long time.

Stegosaurus bones have been found in Colorado, Utah, and Wyoming with *Camptosaurus, Allosaurus,* and *Apatosaurus.*

Stegosaurus

4

The Cretaceous–More Changes, More Dinosaurs

The Cretaceous period began about 135 million years ago. Many changes took place in North America during its 70 million years. This period began with the upheaval of the Cascade and Sierra Nevada mountain ranges in the West. Other portions of western North America sank. A shallow sea covered large areas of the mid-continent. Parts of Saskatchewan, Alberta, and Manitoba in Canada and the Dakotas, Montana, Wyoming, Nebraska, Kansas, Oklahoma, eastern Texas, and eastern Colorado in the United States were under water for most of the Cretaceous period. At one time this vast sea was a thousand miles wide at what is now the Canadian–United States border.

The breakup of the supercontinent entered its final stages. North America pulled farther away from South America and Africa early in the period. Seashores appeared along the eastern coast as the North Atlantic started to form.

Toward the end of the Cretaceous, the North American continent was split by a shallow sea which extended from the Gulf of Mexico to the Arctic Ocean. This sea, the Niobrara, covered most of the Southwest, the Great Plains, and much of the present Rocky Mountain area. North America was still partly connected to Europe on the northeast and to Asia on the northwest. At the very end of the Cretaceous period, the continents were almost completely separated.

During the last 10 or 15 million years of the Cretaceous period the present Rocky Mountains began to rise, swamps and seas drained, and our continent began to look very much as it does today.

The land surfaces of North America were low for most of the Cretaceous age, with small hills, rivers, and lakes. The rivers were faster-flowing than those of the Jurassic. It was a time of building up and wearing down, as drastic erosion took place in the mountains in both the East and the West. Many volcanoes were active in the West.

Great forests and open glades covered areas between inland seas. Both hardwood and evergreen trees grew in the forests. Snakes, lizards, and small mammals such as primitive opossums and shrews scurried among ground-covering ferns and holly on the forest floors. There were thousands of insects. Butterflies were common by the middle of the Cretaceous. Huge 50-foot (15-m) crocodiles lived in swamps among the cattails, reeds, and water lilies. Five-foot (1.5-m) *Champsosaurus* (CHAMP-suh-sawr-us), a sprawling crocodile-like reptile, lived along river and lake margins.

The South and Southwest were covered by grassless tropical jungles and swamps. These swamps left deposits of coal hundreds of feet thick. Most of the Gulf Coast, Mexico, and arctic Canada were covered by the ocean. Baja California looked much as it does now, except that it was thickly wooded and covered with dense vegetation.

The Cretaceous world must have been beautiful. Flowering plants and hardwood trees had become dominant plant forms. Oaks, poplars, walnut, ash, willows, palms, cypress, eucalyptus, laurels, persimmon, magnolia, honeysuckle, and dogwood grew everywhere. But there were also poison ivy and similar plants. Birds were more common than they had been.

Throughout the greater part of the period the climate continued to be mild and, in most places, wet, although there probably were dry seasons. Tropical and subtropical temperatures prevailed as far north as Alaska and Greenland. A cooling trend developed near the end of the Cretaceous, bringing some seasonal changes in temperature. Some scientists believe that a sharp drop in temperature occurred at the very end of the period.

With such a favorable climate and the lush vegetation, the number of animals multiplied rapidly. Even life in the shallow inland seas was abundant and grew to enormous size. A 40-foot (12-m) mosasaur (MOZ-uh-sawr), a marine lizard, was found in Kansas. Other inland sea animals included 18-inch (45-cm) oysters, 14-foot (4.25-m) marine turtles, 25-foot (7.5-m) sharks, and 42-foot (12.5-m) plesiosaurs. Pteranodons (tair-AN-uh-dons) with 20-foot (6-m) wingspreads flew over the inland seas, while many flightless birds swam on their surfaces. Among these were the 6-foot (1.8-m) penguinlike *Hesperornis* (hes-per-OR-nis) and the robin-sized *Ichthyornis* (ik-thee-OR-nis).

Tremendous numbers of dinosaurs lived everywhere on land, from central Canada to Mexico and from New Jersey to California. Huge herds of ornithopods browsed in the forests or grazed in open areas, along rivers or lakes, and along the seashores. With such a plentiful food supply, carnosaurs became enormous. Small theropods hunted in the forests and a few huge sauropods grazed on the tall trees. Toward the end of the period the number of dinosaurs increased, but there were fewer kinds. After the close of the Cretaceous period, there were none.

Early Cretaceous Dinosaurs

We don't know much about the Early Cretaceous dinosaurs. Not many fossils have been found from the first 30 million years of the period. Few exposed areas of Early Cretaceous rock exist in North America. Most of these contain mere fragments and incomplete skeletons. However, enough of these fragments have been found to tell us that small theropods, large carnosaurs, gigantic sauropods, ornithopods, and armored dinosaurs lived in eastern and western North America during that time. Extensive trackways of footprints also tell us that large sauropods and carnosaurs lived in the West. Since there were still land bridges between the continents during most of the period, many of the Early Cretaceous dinosaurs found on other continents may have lived in North America also, but have not yet been found.

DEINONYCHUS
"Terrible Claw"

Deinonychus (dine-ON-ik-us) was an entirely new type of small theropod that lived during the Early Cretaceous period. This vicious little meat eater was about 9 feet (2.75 m) long and only 5 feet (1.5 m) high. It weighed between 150 and 175 pounds (68 and 80 kg).

Deinonychus

Deinonychus walked and ran on powerful, slender hind legs like a large bird, and could probably outrun any other animal of the day. With its streamlined body and long tail stretched rigidly out behind for balance, *Deinonychus* must have looked like an enormously overgrown roadrunner.

Like its coelurosaur ancestors, *Deinonychus* had short front legs, but it had long hands. The front legs were about half as long as the hind legs. They couldn't possibly have been used for walking. Each hand had three powerful clawed fingers that could grasp and slash prey. The wrist joints allowed *Deinonychus* to hold food in its hands like a squirrel.

The feet were quite different from those of earlier theropods. Only two toes were used for walking. The other toe on each foot was armed with a wicked 5-inch (13-cm) sickle-like claw. This agile dinosaur used these claws as weapons to kill prey while standing on one foot and slashing with the other. When not in use, the claws were retracted for protection. Scientists think an animal agile enough to use its claws in this manner must have been warm-blooded.

Deinonychus had a stout neck and a fairly large head. The jaws were filled with sharp, serrated teeth. The eyes were much larger than those of earlier theropods, and *Deinonychus* probably had very good vision. This dinosaur must have been a fairly intelligent animal.

There is evidence that *Deinonychus* may have hunted in packs, but it was perfectly capable of killing an animal larger than itself. Its fossils have been found in Montana near those of an ornithopod, *Tenontosaurus* (see page 67), which may have been a frequent prey.

MICROVENATOR
"Small Hunter"

Microvenator (my-cro-ven-ATE-or) was a turkey-sized coelurosaur that lived in Early Cretaceous North America. Like all coelurosaurs, this descendant of *Coelophysis* was a meat eater. It was very birdlike and probably had a small head, long neck, short front legs with long fingers, strong hind legs, and a long tail.

This tiny, hollow-boned dinosaur weighed between 12 and 15 pounds

(5.5 and 7 kg). It was 2–3 feet (60–90 cm) tall and 3–5 feet (90–150 cm) long.

Microvenator lived in western North America along with *Deinonychus* and *Tenontosaurus.* Its fossils have been found in Montana.

Evidence shows that other coelurosaurs lived during Early Cretaceous times. Coelurosaur tracks found in British Columbia, Canada, have been given the name *Columbosauripus* (ko-lum-bo-SAWR-ih-pus), but no fossilized bones of the animal that made them have been found.

Microvenator

ACROCANTHOSAURUS
"High-spined Lizard"

Acrocanthosaurus (ak-ro-KANTH-uh-sawr-us) was a giant carnosaur that lived in Early Cretaceous North America. This theropod was related to *Allosaurus* and, like *Allosaurus,* had a large head with long jaws and sharp, serrated teeth. *Acrocanthosaurus* was longer and somewhat more slender than *Allosaurus.* It is estimated that this animal was 40 feet (12 m) long. The hind legs were powerful and built for running. The neck and body were short and heavily built.

But the rest of the body was quite different. The spines on the backbone were very long. The neck spines reached a height of 11½ inches (29 cm), and those on the fore part of the tail were more than 17 inches (43 cm) long. *Acrocanthosaurus* is the only North American dinosaur known to have had such high spines. The spines were probably embedded in a thick ridge of muscle.

The purpose of this ridge down the back is not known. Some scientists suggest that it may have developed as an adaptation for carrying the large head.

Acrocanthosaurus bones were found in southeastern Oklahoma. *Tenontosaurus* and sauropod bones were found nearby.

Acrocanthosaurus

PLEUROCOELUS
"Hollow Cavities"

Pleurocoelus (ploor-uh-SEEL-us) is the only North American sauropod from the Early Cretaceous that we know about. An incomplete skeleton was found in the area of Maryland and the District of Columbia. The bones were from a very young animal, estimated to have been only 13½ feet (about 4 m) long. Bones of a much larger sauropod believed to be an adult *Pleurocoelus* were found in Early Cretaceous rock in Texas and also in Montana with *Deinonychus, Tenontosaurus,* and *Microvenator.*

Scientists think that *Pleurocoelus* resembled *Apatosaurus* in size and shape. However, the elephant-like feet were somewhat different. The hind feet had three claws, but the forefeet had no inner claw like that of *Apatosaurus.* The skull was probably quite small. The teeth were long and narrow. The name *Pleurocoelus* refers to hollows in the sides of the vertebrae. This animal is also called *Astrodon* (ASS-tro-don), meaning "star tooth."

A large sauropod left a long line of tracks in the mud along the shore of an ancient Cretaceous sea. These huge tracks were found in Texas near the Paluxy River near Glen Rose, sixty miles southwest of Dallas. They may have been made by *Pleurocoelus.* The animal that made them also had three claws on its hind feet and none on its front feet.

It is known that other sauropods roamed other parts of North America during this period because bits and pieces of their skeletons have been found. Some of these fossil bones were found in southeastern Oklahoma.

Pleurocoelus (Astrodon)

IGUANODON
"Iguana-tooth"

Iguanodon (ig-WAN-o-don) may have lived in North America during Early Cretaceous times. One or two bones found in the western United States may have belonged to this ornithopod. *Iguanodon* has been found on most other continents of the world and most likely lived on this one also.

The European *Iguanodon* was about twice as large as its probable ancestor, the Jurassic *Camptosaurus*. The massively built *Iguanodon* may have weighed 3 tons (2.7 metric tons) or more. It was 25 feet (7.5 m) long and stood 12–15 feet (3.5– 4.5 m) tall. That is tall enough to look into a second-floor window!

Iguanodon

Iguanodon resembled *Camptosaurus* in some ways. Like *Camptosaurus,* it was bipedal. Its body proportions suggest that it probably stood almost upright. *Iguanodon* had relatively short forelimbs. Its hands were equipped with pointed spikelike thumbs that stood at right angles to its other four fingers. The purpose of these spikes is not known. They may have been used as weapons of defense. However, it is possible that *Iguanodon* may have run from danger on its powerful hind legs or used its massive tail to beat off an attacker. Its feet were three-toed, with hooflike claws.

Iguanodon's head was long and flat like that of *Camptosaurus,* but unlike *Camptosaurus, Iguanodon* had a row of closely packed teeth in each jaw, which it used to chop and crush plant fiber. *Iguanodon* probably browsed in herds, and may have eaten primitive flowering plants.

TENONTOSAURUS
"Tendon Lizard"

Tenontosaurus (ten-ON-tuh-sawr-us) was a large ornithopod that lived 116 million years ago during the Early Cretaceous period. This plant eater walked on two legs, but unlike its ancestor *Camptosaurus,* its birdlike feet had only three toes. The short front legs may have been used when feeding, but this use probably wasn't common.

Tenontosaurus was more massive than *Camptosaurus.* It is estimated that this dinosaur measured more than 20 feet (6 m) in length and possibly weighed 2 tons (1.8 metric tons) or more.

In general, *Tenontosaurus* probably resembled the European *Iguanodon,* which lived during the same period. However, *Tenontosaurus* did not have a spiked thumb.

Tenontosaurus may have had protective coloring. It had no other means of protection except a coarse, scaly skin. It was not built for speed and was too large to hide easily. *Deinonychus* was probably its worst enemy. *Tenontosaurus* would have been easy prey for a pack of those vicious animals.

Tenontosaurus must have roamed vast areas of North America. Its fossils

Tenontosaurus

have been found in the Big Horn area of Montana and Wyoming, and also in southeastern Oklahoma. *Acrocanthosaurus* and sauropods were other neighbors.

Ankylosaurs
"Armored Lizards"

Ankylosaurs (ang-KILE-uh-sawrs) appeared in North America during the Cretaceous period at about the time *Stegosaurus* disappeared. These armored dinosaurs were quadrupedal (four-footed) ornithischians. They had small heads, horny beaks, and small, weak teeth. As their hind legs were a little longer than their front legs, they carried their hips high and their heads low.

Ankylosaurs developed a unique way to protect themselves from giant predators. Their bodies were completely encased in bony plates or spines from their heads to their tails. Only their bellies were bare.

These huge animals weighed several tons and, when threatened by danger, probably simply flattened to the ground. The uplands of North America from Baja California to Canada were the home range of these harmless armadillo-like creatures.

Two groups of ankylosaurs existed in North America. One group had long side spines and clubless tails. The other had either no side spines, or very short spines, and clubbed tails.

At least seven different kinds lived in North America during Cretaceous times. *Nodosaurus, Sauropelta, Hoplitosaurus,* and *Silvasaurus* were Early Cretaceous ankylosaurs. Those from the Late Cretaceous period were *Ankylosaurus, Panoplosaurus,* and *Euoplocephalus.*

NODOSAURUS
"Toothless Lizard"

Nodosaurus (NO-doe-sawr-us) is one of the oldest known ankylosaurs, or armored dinosaurs, of North America. Ankylosaurs took the place of *Stegosaurus* early in the Cretaceous period. This huge four-legged plant eater weighed 2 tons (1.8 metric tons), was 17½ feet (5.25 m) long, and stood 6 feet (1.8 m) at the shoulders. It must have looked like an armored tank as it fed on the soft vegetation of the Early Cretaceous world.

Nodosaurus protected itself from vicious predators, such as *Deinonychus* and the gigantic carnosaurs, by growing a suit of armor. The body and head were completely covered by shell-like knobby plates. *Nodosaurus* was further protected by pointed spines down each side of the body and on the back corners of the skull. The tail was protected by bony knobs, but did not have a club as did the tails of later armored dinosaurs. The belly was soft and unprotected, like an armadillo's.

The hind legs of *Nodosaurus* were much longer than the forelegs, so the back was highly arched and the head was carried low. The head is not known, but as in all ankylosaurs the mouth probably ended in a horny beak, and in spite of its name, it probably was not toothless.

Nodosaurus remains have been found in Wyoming.

Stegopelta (steg-uh-PEL-ta) and *Hierosaurus* (HAIR-uh-sawr-us) are two ankylosaurs now considered by some authorities to be the same as *Nodosaurus*. *Stegopelta* was also found in Wyoming. *Hierosaurus* was found in the Niobrara Sea formations of Kansas.

Partial skeletons of other even older Early Cretaceous ankylosaurs have been found. The oldest North American armored dinosaur is named *Sauropelta* (sawr-uh-PEL-tuh), "lizard with shield." Several incomplete skeletons and various bone fragments of this dinosaur have been found in Early Cretaceous rock in Wyoming and Montana, and perhaps in Utah and Colorado. *Sauropelta*'s back and long, clubless tail were covered with rounded horny plates, or scutes. It has been estimated that this animal was 18 feet (about 5.5 m) long and weighed 3 tons (2.7 metric tons) or more.

Another ankylosaur, *Hoplitosaurus* (hop-LEET-uh-sawr-us), "armed lizard," was found in South Dakota. This armored dinosaur may have been similar in appearance to *Polacanthus* (pol-uh-KAN-thus), a European ankylosaur. The back and tail of *Polacanthus* were protected by flattened, rounded plates and two rows of spikes that ran from the neck to the hips. The spikes on the shoulders were longer than the others. A solid bony shield

Nodosaurus

70

protected the hips, and a double row of paired, triangular bony plates ran along the tail.

Silvasaurus (SIL-vuh-sawr-us), "forest lizard," was found in Kansas. This ankylosaur had a longer neck than most. The back and tail were protected by plates, and there were also spikes along its sides.

5

Late Cretaceous– A Population Explosion

Although our knowledge of Early Cretaceous dinosaurs is limited, we have an excellent knowledge of Late Cretaceous dinosaurs. During the Late Cretaceous period, the dinosaur population really exploded into a wide variety of new and different animals. More than twice as many kinds of dinosaurs have been found from the Late Cretaceous period as from any earlier period. The spread of flowering plants around the world produced such an abundant food supply that tremendous numbers of plant eaters evolved to feed upon them.

More new kinds of saurischians have been found from Late Cretaceous rock than from any earlier period. But ornithischians far outnumbered saurischians in North America during the Late Cretaceous.

A few Jurassic saurischians lived on into Cretaceous times. *Allosaurus* and *Diplodocus* continued to exist for a while, but were replaced by new carnosaurs and new sauropods which evolved into forms better suited to their changing environments. Several kinds of coelurosaurs also evolved. Among them were the most intelligent animals of the Mesozoic Era.

However, the ornithischians were the dominant animals of North America during this period. The ornithischians increased not only in numbers, but also in varieties. Whole new genera evolved. *Stegosaurus* lived on into the earliest part of the Late Cretaceous, but soon became extinct, apparently unable to adapt to the changing environment. Many new kinds of ornithischians evolved to take its place. Ornithopods evolved into duckbills, or **hadrosaurs** (see page 95), and curious dome-headed dinosaurs. Two entirely new groups of four-legged plant eaters appeared. These were the armored dinosaurs, or **ankylosaurs,** already discussed, and the horned dinosaurs, or **ceratopsians** (see page 122).

72

Huge herds of duckbills roamed swamps, forest glades, and open plains alongside herds of horned dinosaurs and dome-headed dinosaurs. Armored dinosaurs took the place of *Stegosaurus* in open lands. As time passed, the number and kinds of duckbills increased. Horned dinosaurs, too, became more numerous, and a greater number of varieties appeared.

The Late Cretaceous lasted a very long time. Some dinosaurs lived the full length of the period. Others lived a few million years, then died out and were replaced by new species.

At least fifty-two different kinds of dinosaurs lived during this time. Fewer kinds have been found from the end of the period. That does not necessarily mean that fewer existed; it may be because fewer exposed rocks from that period have been found.

Late Cretaceous Dinosaurs

Ornithomimids
"Bird Mimics"

By the time the last half of the Cretaceous period began, new groups of theropods had evolved in North America. One of these was the "ostrich dinosaurs," or **ornithomimids** (or-nith-o-MEE-mids). The bodies of these descendants of *Coelophysis* looked very much like those of ostriches. They had the same long, flexible necks and small, flat heads with birdlike beaks, and they walked on two long, slender legs. But ornithomimids had long, reptilian tails. They also had well-developed arms and hands instead of wings, and they did not have feathers.

All ornithomimids had lightly built bodies and hollow bones. They were fleet-footed animals. Like ostriches, they ran on their toes, but had three toes instead of two. The front legs, or arms, of ornithomimids were long and clawed.

These coelurosaurs must have filled a very important role in their ecological system, because they and their relatives existed for millions of years, to the very end of the Cretaceous period. Perhaps these very specialized dinosaurs helped control reptile and mammal populations by using their large brains, grasping hands, and great agility to steal eggs and capture young. They also must have assisted the spread of flowering plants by eating their fruit and distributing the seeds.

ORNITHOMIMUS
"Bird Imitator" and
STRUTHIOMIMUS
"Ostrich Mimic"

These two dinosaurs looked very much alike. Some scientists think they are one and the same. Others consider them to be entirely different kinds of animals. *Ornithomimus* (or-nith-o-MIME-us) was found first, but little is known about that animal.

Struthiomimus (strooth-ee-o-MIME-us) was just a little larger and heavier than an ostrich. It stood 7 feet (about 2 m) tall and was 12 feet (3.5 m) long from the end of the beak to the tip of the tail. *Ornithomimus* may have stood 8 feet (2.5 m) tall and measured up to 15 feet (4.5 m) long. Most of the length of these animals was in their ostrich-like necks and their long tails. The tail of *Struthiomimus* was 3 feet (90 cm) longer than its very short body.

These fleet-footed dinosaurs could probably run as fast as an ostrich, and therefore may have been warm-blooded. Their long legs were slender but powerful. A horny beak covered the toothless jaws of their small, flat heads. Their brain cases were quite large, and scientists think they must have been at least as intelligent as ostriches.

Although their eyes were very large and may have been able to see well in dim light, these graceful little dinosaurs were probably day hunters. They may have been omnivorous like ostriches—that is, they may have eaten both

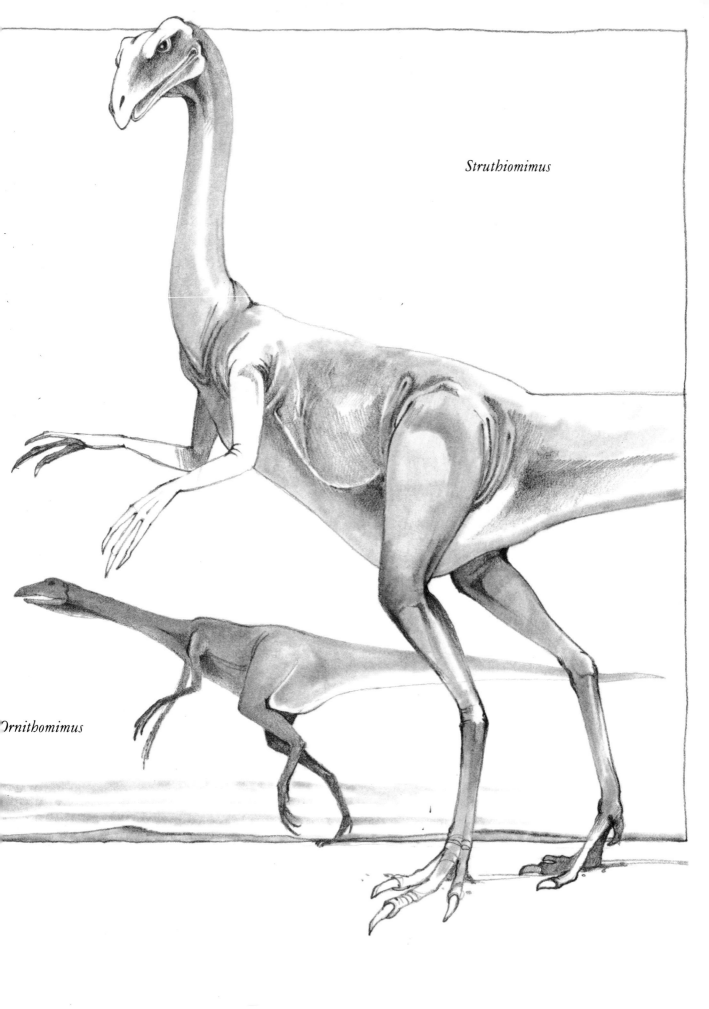

Struthiomimus

Ornithomimus

plants and animals. They possibly dined on fruit, small reptiles, insects, and eggs of other dinosaurs. Their strong front legs were equipped with three long fingers that had claws like a bear's. The claws may have been used to rip apart logs, or rake away ground cover to get at insects, or dig up reptile eggs.

The greatest protection of these small dinosaurs was probably their tremendous speed. Few other dinosaurs could run faster. Too, their exceptionally good eyesight helped them spot the giant carnosaurs who were their worst enemies. They may have lived in herds for more protection. Some scientists suggest that the young may have been well developed at birth (or when hatched) and may have received parental care until they were large enough to fend for themselves.

Ornithomimus and *Struthiomimus* have been found in many regions of western United States and Canada. Like ostriches, they probably preferred open plains, but sometimes may have roamed the humid coastal swamps and forests of Late Cretaceous North America. Their neighbors were duckbills, horned dinosaurs, and giant carnosaurs.

DROMICEIOMIMUS
"Emu Mimic"

Dromiceiomimus (drom-ice-ee-uh-MIME-us), another of the "ostrich dinosaurs," was the most common type found in the hardwood forests of western Canada in Late Cretaceous times. This dinosaur was about as big as a medium-sized ostrich. It measured 10 feet (3 m) from the tip of the beak to the end of the tail, and weighed about 175 pounds (80 kg). *Dromiceiomimus* had the same long neck, birdlike beak, and long, slender legs as other "ostrich dinosaurs." The eyes were huge—larger than those of any other known land animal. The brain was larger than that of an ostrich. *Dromiceiomimus* was possibly one of the most intelligent animals of the Cretaceous.

Although this dinosaur probably couldn't dodge as well as the ostrich of today, it probably could outrun one. An ostrich can run 50 miles (80 km) per hour. The tremendous speed of *Dromiceiomimus* combined with its mental ability and keen eyesight made it very hard to capture. These were excellent defenses against the giant carnosaur *Albertosaurus (Gorgosaurus),* which lived in the same area at the same time.

Dromiceiomimus may have lived in herds or flocks. The claws on their three very long fingers were probably used for raking leaves and twigs from the forest floor to uncover small ground animals, which they ate.

It has been suggested that the *Dromiceiomimus* young may have been born alive, but this is not widely accepted. However, scientists do think that the parents took care of the babies, because they have found an adult buried with two young *Dromiceiomimus.* This dinosaur certainly must have had the mental capacity to do this.

Dromiceiomimus fossils have been found in Alberta, Canada. This animal lived in the same areas as huge duckbills, horned dinosaurs, and other "ostrich dinosaurs."

Dromiceiomimus and young

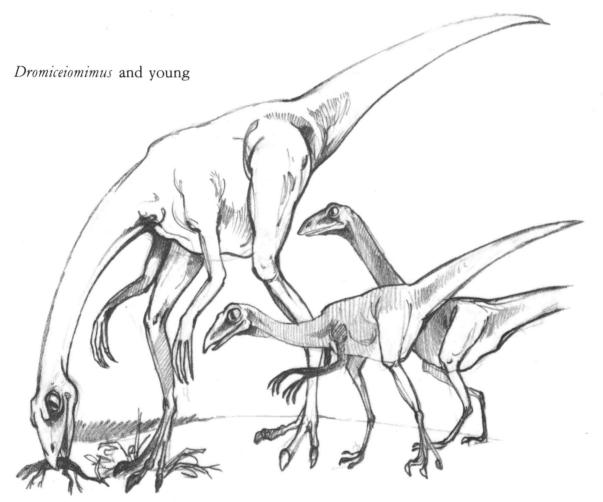

DROMAEOSAURUS
"Swift Lizard"

Dromaeosaurus (drom-ee-uh-SAWR-us), a descendant of *Deinonychus,* was the first of another group of small theropods called dromaeosaurs. This dinosaur lived in western North America during later Cretaceous times, several million years after *Deinonychus.*

Like the "ostrich dinosaurs," *Dromaeosaurus* walked on two legs and was very fleet-footed. It probably could run almost as fast as *Struthiomimus.* The hind legs were strong and powerful. Possibly it was warm-blooded.

Although this man-sized little theropod weighed no more than 100 pounds (45 kg), it was a flesh eater and a vicious killer. The head, which measured 8 inches (20 cm), was larger than that of *Struthiomimus.* It had long jaws that were lined with razor-sharp, finely serrated teeth. In addition, the inner toe of each foot was equipped with a 3-inch (8-cm) talon like an eagle's, and like that of *Deinonychus.* Probably *Dromaeosaurus* used these built-in "switchblades" to cut open the stomachs of prey while holding them in its hands. Each hand had three long, grasping fingers.

In Mongolia, scientists have found a very close relative of *Dromaeosaurus* tangled in a death struggle with a calf-sized horned dinosaur, *Protoceratops* (see page 125). This dinosaur, *Velociraptor* (veh-loss-ih-RAP-tor), died with its hands gripping the head of the *Protoceratops* and a sickle-like talon buried in the belly of its prey.

The neck of *Dromaeosaurus* was rather long, but thick and powerful like that of a carnosaur. The front legs, however, were much longer than those of carnosaurs. Probably the long, tapering tail was held rigidly behind to counterbalance the head when *Dromaeosaurus* was running or walking.

Dromaeosaurus had a very broad skull and a large brain. It also had large eyes and probably had very good eyesight. This meat eater must have been a formidable creature with its agility, speed, and greater mental capacity. This dinosaur may have been more dangerous than *Tyrannosaurus* if it hunted in packs.

Remains of *Dromaeosaurus* have been found in western Canada in the same areas where the "ostrich dinosaurs," duckbills, and horned and armored dinosaurs have been found. It existed to the very end of the Cretaceous period.

Dromaeosaurus

STENONYCHOSAURUS
"Narrow-clawed Lizard"

Stenonychosaurus (sten-on-IK-uh-sawr-us), a close relative of *Dromaeosaurus,* lived during the same time period as that animal. Like *Dromaeosaurus, Stenonychosaurus* was two-legged and hollow-boned.

This small theropod was no more than 6 feet (1.8 m) long and weighed about 60 pounds (27 kg). The head was fairly large, measuring 9 inches (23 cm) long in adults. The snout was triangular and the bill-like muzzle was lined with sharp, serrated teeth. *Stenonychosaurus* had exceptionally good eyesight. The distance between the eyes was unusually great. Widely spaced eyes make it possible to judge distances very accurately. The huge 2-inch (5-cm) eyes were as large as those of any land animal living today, and probably provided good night vision.

Some scientists think *Stenonychosaurus* was the most intelligent of all the dinosaurs. It must have been at least as smart as an emu, as its brain was larger. And of all birds, the emu has the largest brain in proportion to body weight.

This little flesh eater was a very active predator. It probably could run faster than *Dromaeosaurus.* Although the sickle-like claws on its feet were smaller than those of *Dromaeosaurus,* its well-coordinated hands could easily catch and hold prey. The claws indicate that *Stenonychosaurus* probably caught prey animals larger than itself.

Stenonychosaurus may have hunted mammals by night, or at least at twilight. This is especially likely if it was warm-blooded, as some scientists believe. No one knows whether *Stenonychosaurus* had developed an insulating covering for its body such as fur or feathers, but some scientists think it may have.

Stenonychosaurus fossils have been found in western Canada. Like emus of today, these animals may have lived in herds and cared for their young.

There may have been many more of this type of dinosaur. A close relative of *Stenonychosaurus* lived in Mongolia. *Saurornithoides* (sawr-or-nith-OY-deez) so closely resembles *Stenonychosaurus* that some scientists think the two may be the same.

Scientists have found forty dinosaur eggs in Montana. Along with the eggs were found fragments of bone and teeth, indicating that the dinosaurs which laid the eggs may have been carnivorous, perhaps a small theropod similar to *Stenonychosaurus.* The eggs are 6 inches (15 cm) long and 4 inches (10 cm) wide, and have a black, pebbled exterior. The eggs were found in clusters or nests, leading scientists to believe that adult dinosaurs gave more care to their young than was once thought. If these eggs prove to be theropod eggs, they will be the first theropod eggs ever found.

A single coelurosaur tooth was found in the same area of Montana in 1856. It was given the name *Troödon* (TRUE-o-don), which means "wound tooth." Perhaps the tooth and the eggs both belong to the same animal.

We know that other small theropods lived during the Late Cretaceous, because tracks and fragments of skeletons have been found in western North America. So far, not enough bones have been found for us to know exactly how the animals looked.

Stenonychosaurus

DASPLETOSAURUS
"Frightful Lizard"

Daspletosaurus (das-PLEE-tuh-sawr-us), a large Late Cretaceous carnosaur, lived at the same time and in the same areas of Canada as *Albertosaurus (Gorgosaurus)*. But this dinosaur was not so plentiful.

This heavy-bodied relative of *Tyrannosaurus* measured 30 feet (9 m) from the tip of the huge head to the end of the long tail. It may have weighed 7,000 pounds (3,150 kg). Like *Albertosaurus,* it was a two-legged meat eater with short arms. The teeth were long and serrated, and the legs were probably long and powerful.

Daspletosaurus lived in marshlands near streams. *Champsosaurus,* a large, sprawling reptile, may have been a favorite prey.

Daspletosaurus

ALBERTOSAURUS
"Lizard from Alberta"

This fearsome killer was "king of the jungle" in its day. It was the most abundant of the large carnosaurs of Late Cretaceous times. A close relative, and perhaps ancestor, of *Tyrannosaurus,* it is best known as *Gorgosaurus* (GOR-guh-sawr-us), "terrible lizard." However, *Albertosaurus* (al-BER-tuh-sawr-us) is the correct name because this was the name first given to this dinosaur. *Gorgosaurus* was given to fossils found later that proved to be the same animal as *Albertosaurus.*

Albertosaurus (Gorgosaurus) was a slimmer and lighter animal than its ancestor, *Allosaurus.* A large *Albertosaurus* weighed about 3 tons (2.7 metric tons) and stood 7 to 11 feet (2 to 3.3 m) tall at the hips. It measured between 25 and 35 feet (7.5 and 10.5 m) from the end of the nose to the tip of the tail. Earlier species were somewhat smaller than those that lived millions of years later, near the end of the Cretaceous period.

This aggressive theropod walked on two long and powerful hind legs. Probably the fastest runner of the large dinosaurs of the Late Cretaceous, it was a well-armed predator. Its feet were equipped with three long talons. The front legs were short—not much longer than a man's arms—and had only two fingers. These "arms" could not have been used for walking or capturing prey, but they must have served some purpose because their muscles were well developed and the claws on the fingers were quite long.

A short, stout neck supported the huge 22-inch (55-cm) head. The mouth of *Albertosaurus* was filled with long, sharp, back-curving teeth. To kill, it used the great talon-bearing feet and large serrated teeth. Its favorite food was probably one of the many neighboring duck-billed dinosaurs.

Large numbers of *Albertosaurus (Gorgosaurus)* roamed the thickly forested lowlands of western North America. Their bones and teeth have been found from Canada to Baja California. Horned dinosaurs also roamed this area. Like all theropods, *Albertosaurus (Gorgosaurus)* had a flexible shield of riblike bones beneath the skin of the chest and belly. This shield, which looked a little like the bone breastplates worn by some American Indians, helped to protect it from the stabs of the horned dinosaurs.

Albertosaurus (Gorgosaurus) lived almost to the end of the Late Cretaceous period.

Albertosaurus (Gorgosaurus)

DRYPTOSAURUS
"Tearing Lizard"

Dryptosaurus (DRIP-tuh-sawr-us) is the only giant carnosaur from the Cretaceous period that has been found in eastern North America. This formidable meat eater had daggerlike teeth and 8-inch (20-cm) claws like the talons of an eagle. The body and head probably resembled those of *Albertosaurus (Gorgosaurus)* and *Tyrannosaurus.* The arms were only about a third as long as the legs. *Dryptosaurus* was, nonetheless, a ferocious hunter, and probably preyed upon the duckbills that lived in the same area. Its exact size is not known because a complete skeleton has not been found. The incomplete skeleton of this theropod was found in New Jersey.

Dryptosaurus was originally named *Laelaps* (LIE-laps), meaning "leaper." Then it was discovered that another animal (not a dinosaur) had already been given that name, so it was renamed *Dryptosaurus.*

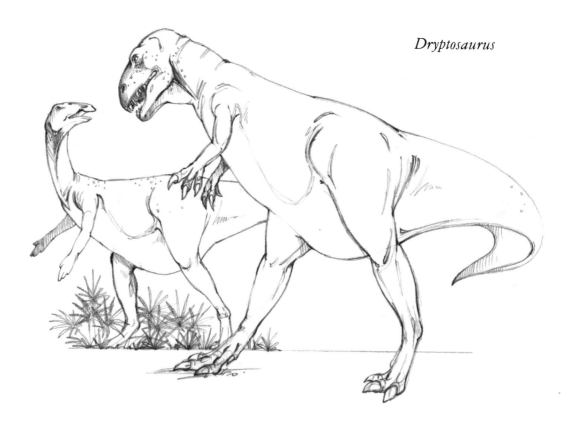

Dryptosaurus

TYRANNOSAURUS
"Tyrant Lizard"

Tyrannosaurus (tie-RAN-uh-sawr-us) was the last of the gigantic carnosaurs in North America. It was well named, for this enormous meat eater ruled the earth during the last 4 or 5 million years of the Cretaceous period.

This largest known carnosaur measured 47 feet (14.5 m) from the tip of the nose to the end of the tail, and when standing upright was 18½ feet (about 5.5 m) tall. It weighed more than 5 tons (4.5 metric tons)!

The enormous head, which was even larger than that of *Allosaurus,* was more than 4 feet (1.2 m) from front to back. The jaws were 3 feet (90 cm) long and armed with 6-inch (15-cm) saberlike teeth. The teeth were 1 inch (2.5 cm) wide, curved, and finely serrated on each side like spear points.

Like all theropods, *Tyrannosaurus* was two-legged. Although it may have stood upright sometimes, it probably walked or ran bent over with the giant tail stretched out to balance the huge head and body. This gigantic theropod may not have been able to run as fast as *Albertosaurus (Gorgosaurus)*, but its legs were longer and more powerful. *Tyrannosaurus* needed its greater leg strength to capture the larger horned dinosaurs and swifter duckbills of the period.

Tyrannosaurus's great birdlike feet had three forward-pointing toes and one reversed toe. The forward toes were armed with 8-inch (20-cm) talons, and like an eagle, this ferocious killer used its jaws and talons to capture and kill prey. One blow from either would have seriously injured anything. *Tyrannosaurus* could open its mouth extremely wide and could swallow huge hunks of meat whole.

The "tyrant lizard" couldn't possibly have caught food with its tiny, two-fingered arms. They were even smaller than the arms of *Albertosaurus.* *Tyrannosaurus* couldn't even scratch its chin with those short 30-inch (75-cm) arms. But they must have been used for something, for they, too, were armed with long, strong claws.

Food was no problem for this gigantic meat eater. There were tremendous numbers of large, plant-eating dinosaurs living nearby. A hungry *Tyrannosaurus* may even have taken on *Triceratops* when nothing else was available. But it is more likely that *Tyrannosaurus* preferred the huge, unarmed duck-billed *Anatosaurus* or the dome-headed *Pachycephalosaurus,*

Tyrannosauru.

which were quite plentiful. *Tyrannosaurus* may have hunted in packs or family groups, probably killing the prey immediately. But it may have torn off huge hunks of flesh while the animal was still alive, in the manner that some dogs attack sheep.

Tyrannosaurus has been found in the northern regions of western North America.

Many other Late Cretaceous carnosaurs may have lived in North America. New evidence of this has recently been discovered in Baja California. Fragments of a giant carnosaur named *Labocania* (lab-o-KAY-nee-uh) were found there. This carnosaur was more massive than most carnosaurs, but smaller than *Tyrannosaurus.*

ALAMOSAURUS
"Alamo Lizard"

Only two sauropods known to have lived in North America during Late Cretaceous times have been identified. *Alamosaurus* is one of these. This dinosaur was the last of the North American sauropods we know about. It lived to the very end of the Mesozoic Era. The name *Alamosaurus* (AL-a-mo-sawr-us) refers to the Ojo Alamo rock formation in New Mexico, from which it was collected.

Although huge, among sauropods this plant eater was medium-sized, probably around 50 feet (15 m) from the end of the nose to the tip of the tail.

Alamosaurus is known only from fragments, but is thought to have resembled *Diplodocus.* It had a long neck and tail and walked on four elephant-like feet. The front legs were three fourths the length of the hind legs.

Alamosaurus roamed the Late Cretaceous tropical forests from Utah to Texas. Its fossils have been found in Texas, New Mexico, Utah, and perhaps Wyoming.

A partial skeleton of the second Late Cretaceous sauropod was found in southeastern Missouri. This sauropod is named *Parrosaurus* (PAR-uh-sawr-us), "Parr's lizard," in honor of Albert Parr, who was director of Yale's

Peabody Museum of Natural History and, later, of the American Museum of Natural History in New York City. *Parrosaurus* is believed to be a descendant of *Camarasaurus* and probably resembled that dinosaur.

Alamosaurus

PARKSOSAURUS
"Parks's Lizard"

Parksosaurus (PARKS-uh-sawr-us) was named in honor of W. A. Parks, Canadian dinosaur collector and researcher. This small ornithopod lived with others of its kind in the bushy undergrowth of evergreen forests during Late Cretaceous times.

This little plant eater was 7 feet (about 2 m) long and weighed 150 pounds (68 kg). It was a relative of, and resembled, *Camptosaurus.* Like *Camptosaurus, Parksosaurus* probably walked on two legs more often than on all fours, but it was capable of traveling both ways. The hind legs and toes were long, and the front legs were short but strong. *Parksosaurus* was probably a fast runner and used speed to escape *Albertosaurus (Gorgosaurus).*

The long neck of *Parksosaurus* supported a small head which ended in a duckbill-like snout. The eyes were large for an ornithopod.

Parksosaurus fossils have been found in Montana and in Alberta, Canada, near those of duckbills and the "ostrich dinosaurs."

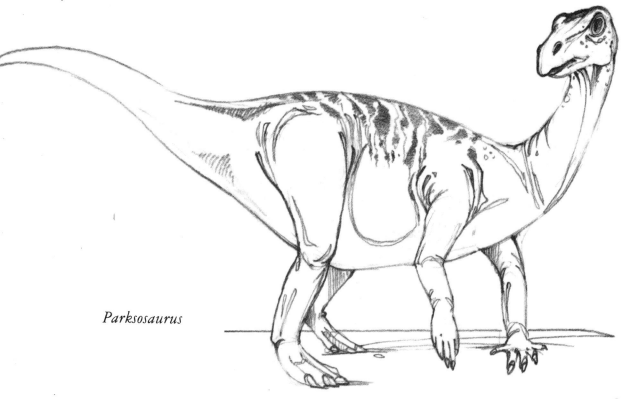

Parksosaurus

THESCELOSAURUS
"Marvelous Lizard"

The bird-hipped dinosaur *Thescelosaurus* (THESS-uh-lo-sawr-us) was a contemporary of *Parksosaurus,* and resembled *Camptosaurus* and *Parksosaurus* in general appearance.

Thescelosaurus measured 12 feet (3.5 m) from snout to end of tail, and weighed about 550 pounds (250 kg). With its rather plump body, small head, and long tail, this ornithopod was a strange-looking combination.

This medium-sized plant eater probably walked on all fours more often than other small ornithopods. The front legs were short, but strong and well developed. Pointed, hooflike claws covered the tips of the five fingers. Each back foot had four toes. *Thescelosaurus* probably carried its body in a horizontal position even when walking on only two legs. The long tail balanced the body weight. *Thescelosaurus* was probably a swift runner. Speed was its best protection from *Tyrannosaurus.*

Thescelosaurus grazed in underbrush near the banks of rivers and streams in Late Cretaceous times. Its fossils have been found in Saskatchewan and Alberta in Canada, and in Wyoming, South Dakota, and Montana in the United States. *Anatosaurus, Triceratops,* and *Ankylosaurus* lived nearby.

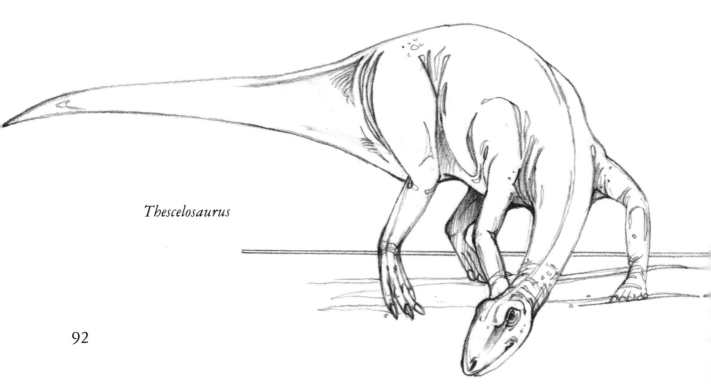

Thescelosaurus

STEGOCERAS
"Covered Horn"

Stegoceras (steg-OSS-air-us) was an unusual ornithopod. This strange animal belonged to a group known as the "dome-headed" dinosaurs. Its broad body was topped by an unusually thick skull. Three inches (8 cm) of solid bone covered the brain. Several small spikes fringed the back of its head. Unlike other ornithopods, *Stegoceras* did not have a beak. The jaws were lined with short, weak teeth. It probably ate only soft ground plants.

It is estimated that this man-sized ornithopod was 5–6 feet (1.5–1.8 m) long and weighed about 120 pounds (55 kg). Its skull measured 7½ inches

Stegoceras

93

(19 cm). This fleet-footed dinosaur probably ran on two legs with its broad body held horizontally and its long, slender tail extended. It had five short toes on its short front legs and four longer toes on its strong hind legs.

Stegoceras probably lived and grazed in hilly upland country, where it occupied the same ecological niche in the Cretaceous world that sheep and goats do today.

Stegoceras bones have been found in northwestern North America.

PACHYCEPHALOSAURUS
"Thick-headed Lizard"

Pachycephalosaurus (pak-ee-SEF-uh-lo-sawr-us) was another of the "dome-headed" dinosaurs. It was a close relative of *Stegoceras,* but lived a few million years later during the last part of the Cretaceous period.

We don't know how large *Pachycephalosaurus* was because only skulls of this animal have been found. However, if the rest of its body matched its skull, it may have been as much as three times as large as *Stegoceras.* The skull of *Pachycephalosaurus* measured 26 inches (65 cm). The solid bone covering its brain was 9 inches (23 cm) thick. Like *Stegoceras,* instead of a horny beak it had jaws lined with sharp teeth. Wartlike knobs and spikes up to 5 inches (13 cm) long fringed the "dome" and decorated the small nose.

No one knows the purpose of the thick dome or spikes. It has been suggested that this harmless plant eater may have been a herding animal. Perhaps males fought duels by butting heads, like mountain goats, to defend territories or to compete for mates. Leaders may have defended their herds by turning to butt an attacker while the rest of the herd fled.

We know nothing about the body of *Pachycephalosaurus,* but it was probably a two-legged animal that ran with its body held horizontally and with its tail extended, like *Stegoceras.*

This Late Cretaceous dinosaur roamed the open plains in western Canada and Montana. It may also have ranged into mountain or hill areas where *Tyrannosaurus* did not hunt. *Pachycephalosaurus* was a neighbor of *Thescelosaurus.*

Hadrosaurs
"Bulky Lizards"

Hadrosaurs (HAD-ruh-sawrs), the duck-billed dinosaurs, were the most diverse and abundant type of dinosaur in Late Cretaceous North America. These descendants of *Camptosaurus* roamed North America from Mexico to northern Canada and from New Jersey to Baja California. Their fossilized remains make up about seventy-five percent of all land animal kinds that have been found.

Hadrosaurs are believed to have evolved from an Asian iguanodont, *Probactrosaurus* (pro-bak-truh-SAWR-us). From Asia, they spread all over the world. Many different kinds of hadrosaurs evolved. All hadrosaurs, or duckbills, had similar heavy bodies and long heads with broad, flat, horny bills, but they varied greatly in the way the tops of their heads developed. Hadrosaurs are best known for their crests, but not all had crests. Some were flat-headed. Some had crests of solid bone, and some had hollow crests.

There were also significant differences in the bodies of the two main subfamilies, so that scientists can determine to which kind a new discovery belongs even if the top of the head is missing. **Hadrosaurines** had long, slender limbs, relatively low spines on their pelvic vertebrae, ridged or slightly expanded bills, long, straight lower jaws, and either no crests at all or crests of solid bone. **Lambeosaurines** had shorter, robust limbs, high spines on their pelvic vertebrae, greatly expanded bills with shorter, downward-curved lower jaws, and a strange variety of hollow crests equipped with nasal passages.

The purpose of these crests is not known. They may have been resonating chambers to make voices louder (hadrosaurs probably had very loud voices like alligators and crocodiles). The crests may have improved their sense of smell. As hadrosaurs probably browsed almost continuously, the hollow crests may have allowed them to breathe while eating. Or the crests may have helped identify species, as do the horns of antelopes. Four to eight species of hadrosaurs existed at any one time during the Late Cretaceous. Scientists think that many varieties grazed together, just as many kinds of antelope do today in Africa. Fossils of several different kinds of hadrosaurs have been found close together in western North America, so perhaps they needed a method of distinguishing species.

95

Pachycephalosaurus

Like all ornithopods, hadrosaurs were bipedal. They were fairly fleet on their two feet but probably couldn't run as swiftly as a horse. Their strong legs were twice as long as their slender, four-fingered front limbs. The tips of their toes and fingers were covered with hoofs instead of claws. These "graceful" animals probably ran or walked with their backs horizontal and their flat, crocodile-like tails stretched out behind.

Because their forefeet were webbed, it was once thought that these animals were water dwellers, eating only soft water plants. Some scientists now believe that they were land foragers that went into the water to escape predators. They were probably good swimmers, as are most land animals of today.

Fossilized stomach contents show that hadrosaurs ate leaves, twigs, and pine needles. Although the jaws were toothless in front, the back of each jaw was lined with several rows of teeth packed close together. Some species had up to five hundred teeth on each side of the upper and lower jaws—two thousand teeth altogether! As old teeth wore down, they were pushed out and replaced by new ones. These teeth were well suited for grinding hard, fibrous food. Well-developed cheek muscles held the food in while it was being chewed.

Hadrosaurs had tough, leathery skin with a rough texture. Keen eyesight and hearing and a good sense of smell were probably their best protection. By getting an early warning of an enemy's approach, they could flee to safety.

Hadrosaurs may have been warm-blooded. They were egg-laying animals and possibly took some care of the young until they were old enough to fend for themselves. Young animals did not develop crests until they were half grown.

Sixteen kinds of hadrosaurs have been found in North America. Ten were hadrosaurines—the crestless or solid-crested variety. Six were lambeosaurines, or hollow-crested.

CLAOSAURUS
"Broken Lizard"

Claosaurus (CLAY-o-sawr-us), one of the oldest known hadrosaurs of North America, may have been the ancestor of all other hadrosaurs on this continent. In some ways *Claosaurus* resembled its ancestor, *Iguanodon.*

Claosaurus had a narrow, medium-length head. Its teeth, which grew only in the back part of its jaws, were more primitive than the teeth of other duckbills. The hind feet were more like those of an *Iguanodon* than those of other hadrosaurs. Measuring only 10–12 feet (3–3.5 m) in length, *Claosaurus* was also smaller than later hadrosaurs.

This duckbill had a typical hadrosaurian build, however, with a heavy body, short front limbs, strong legs, and a heavy, powerful tail equipped with many rodlike tendons. *Claosaurus* probably held its tail stretched out behind as it ran on its two powerful legs. The body was carried horizontally, with the head up. *Claosaurus* may have used its short, slender arms to balance the sway of its shoulders. The long fingers and toes were covered with hoof-like nails or claws.

Claosaurus

Claosaurus probably depended on speed for protection against *Tyrannosaurus.* It grazed on plants and shrubs along the shores of the Niobrara, the great inland sea that covered most of the central part of North America during Late Cretaceous times. Its fossils have been found in Kansas and Wyoming.

The oldest known hadrosaur from North America is a juvenile hadrosaurine that was found in Mississippi. This animal—not yet named—was similar to *Kritosaurus* or *Lophorhothon.*

HADROSAURUS
"Bulky Lizard" and
KRITOSAURUS
"Noble Lizard"

Hadrosaurus (HAD-ruh-sawr-us) was the first dinosaur skeleton discovered in North America. Its nearly complete skeleton was found in New Jersey in 1858. This duckbill has since been found in many places in North America. *Hadrosaurus* developed early in the Late Cretaceous and lived until the last part of the period. Then it was replaced by another duckbill, *Anatosaurus. Kritosaurus* also developed early in the Late Cretaceous period. *Kritosaurus* (KRIT-uh-sawr-us) was quite similar to *Hadrosaurus.* Although some scientists consider these two dinosaurs to be the same, others do not.

Both were about the same size. *Hadrosaurus* measured 30 feet (9 m) long, but its tail made up most of its length. It stood 15–18 feet (4.5–5.5 m) tall when standing erect, or about 10 feet (3 m) tall at the hips. These animals probably weighed about 3 tons (2.7 metric tons).

Both of these hadrosaurs are considered flat-headed duckbills, although the top of *Hadrosaurus*'s head has never been found. *Kritosaurus* had a broad, flat head, but a low ridge of bone in front of the eyes gave the animal a humped or "Roman" nose. Its face was long and narrow, ending in a broad ducklike bill. The jaws were lined at the back with rows of hundreds of grinding teeth.

Hadrosaurus and *Kritosaurus* were bipedal like all duckbills, but they

Kritosaurus

Hadrosaurus

probably walked on all fours when feeding. Their legs were long and strong, and were twice the length of their slender forelimbs. They carried their heavy bodies horizontally. *Kritosaurus* may have had a fleshy ridge 4–5 inches (10–13 cm) high down the middle of its back from the top of the head to the tip of the tail.

These "graceful" animals browsed on pine needles, leaves, and twigs in dry coastal plains with large herds of other duckbills. This herding, along with keen eyesight and hearing and moderate speed, protected them from attacks by *Albertosaurus (Gorgosaurus)*.

Hadrosaurus and *Kritosaurus* fossils have been found in such widely scattered areas as New Mexico, New Jersey, and Montana, and Alberta, Canada. These animals probably ranged throughout the continent.

BRACHYLOPHOSAURUS "Short-crested Lizard"

Brachylophosaurus (brak-ee-LO-fuh-sawr-us) was similar to its cousin *Kritosaurus,* but had a larger hump on its nose and a thin, bony plate over the top of its head. This flat-headed hadrosaur lived in lush upland forests of western Canada during Late Cretaceous times, 74 million years ago. It browsed with large herds of other kinds of hadrosaurs—maybe with *Hadrosaurus,* for they lived during the same time period. *Brachylophosaurus* probably ate leaves and twigs of flowering plants.

Brachylophosaurus was 16½ feet (about 5 m) tall from the top of its head to the ground. The face was deep and narrow, somewhat like that of a horse, but with a rounded bill. The hump on the nose formed a broad, flat, bony shield over the front of the skull. *Brachylophosaurus* may have fought with others of its kind to establish territorial rights, as goats and deer do. It may have stood more erect when butting than did the dome-headed dinosaurs.

Brachylophosaurus may have depended upon speed to avoid *Albertosaurus (Gorgosaurus)*. It is unlikely that the shield on its head provided any protection against such a formidable enemy.

A partial skeleton of a similar hadrosaur was found in Alabama. It was named *Lophorhothon* (lo-for-HO-thon), meaning "crested nose," because,

Brachylophosaurus

like *Brachylophosaurus,* it had a hump above the nostrils, in front of the eyes. It is estimated that this animal, which appears to be a juvenile, was between 12 and 15 feet (3.5 and 4.5 m) long. An adult would have been larger.

EDMONTOSAURUS
"Edmonton Lizard"

Edmontosaurus (ed-MON-tuh-sawr-us) was named for the Edmonton rock formation from which it was recovered. It was the most abundant animal in the swampy forested areas of Alberta, Canada, about 73 million years ago. This duck-billed dinosaur was kin to *Kritosaurus,* and like *Kritosaur-*

us had a heavy body, long, strong legs, short, slender forelimbs, and possibly a frill running down the back and tail. Its horselike head had a long, narrow nose. However, unlike *Kritosaurus, Edmontosaurus* had no hump on its nose. The nose was flat like that of *Claosaurus,* but the front of the jaws had developed into a broad, spoonlike beak.

Edmontosaurus was larger than *Hadrosaurus,* measuring 32 feet (10 m) or more and probably weighing 3 or 4 tons (2.7 or 3.6 metric tons).

It may have browsed on leaves of cypress and broad-leafed trees 10 feet (3 m) above the ground, while other hadrosaurs browsed at lower levels. *Hadrosaurus, Saurolophus, Hypacrosaurus,* and *Parasaurolophus* are other hadrosaurs that lived in Canada during the same period.

Albertosaurus (Gorgosaurus) also shared the environment of *Edmontosaurus.* Like all hadrosaurs, *Edmontosaurus* probably depended upon speed to avoid capture. Its keen senses of hearing and sight would have given it plenty of warning at the approach of danger.

Edmontosaurus

ANATOSAURUS
"Duck Lizard"

Anatosaurus (ah-NAT-uh-sawr-us) is one of the best known of the North American duckbills. It is also called *Trachodon* (TRAK-o-don), meaning "rough tooth." Two skeletons with the mummified skin impressions on them were found in Wyoming. Only the color of this animal is not known.

Like its ancestor *Edmontosaurus*, *Anatosaurus* had no crest or hump on its nose. The head and body resembled that of *Edmontosaurus*, but this duckbill was smaller. It weighed about 3½ tons (3.15 metric tons), was 30 feet (9 m) long, and stood 14 feet (4.25 m) tall.

This hadrosaur was a graceful animal. Like all hadrosaurs, it was bipedal and ran rapidly with tail outstretched. The long, strong legs had large, three-toed feet, the toes ending in broad, rounded hoofs. The slender forelimbs had four-fingered hands. A webbed "mitten" of skin joined the fingers. The long tail was deep, strong, and flattened like that of a crocodile.

The horny beak was very broad and was ridged lengthwise like a duck's bill. It was broader and more spatulate, or spoon-shaped, than that of *Edmontosaurus*. Males had broader bills than females or juveniles. There were no teeth in the bill, but both upper and lower jaws were lined with several hundred prism-shaped teeth arranged in alternating rows—two thousand or more in all. The teeth kept growing as long as the animal lived, and were replaced as rapidly as they wore out. *Anatosaurus*'s eyes were large, and the nostrils were high on the snout. *Anatosaurus* probably had very good eyesight, hearing, and sense of smell.

The body was covered with a leathery skin similar to that of a gila monster. It was textured with small bumps, or tubercles. Possibly a small frill, or fleshy ridge, ran down the back and tail.

From the contents of the mummified stomach, we know that *Anatosaurus* ate shrubs and evergreen needles. It probably browsed in lush tropical forests along riverbanks. Maybe these animals closed their beaks over branches and stripped off the leaves and shoots the way giraffes do.

Anatosaurus probably depended upon speed and keen eyesight and hearing to avoid *Tyrannosaurus*. Its flat, crocodile-like tail made *Anatosaurus* a good swimmer. When threatened by danger, it may sometimes have taken to water and swum to safety.

Anatosaurus (Trachodon)

One of the last dinosaurs, this flat-headed hadrosaur lived to the very end of the Cretaceous period, along with *Triceratops* and *Tyrannosaurus*. *Anatosaurus* was a successful animal. Although it didn't evolve until near the end of the age of dinosaurs, it nonetheless lived several million years.

Anatosaurus remains have been found in Wyoming, Montana, and Alberta, Canada.

MAIASAURA
"Maternal Lizard"

Maiasaura (mah-ee-uh-SAWR-uh) lived in Montana during the Late Cretaceous, between 70 and 80 million years ago. This duck-billed dinosaur was an important discovery. It is called "maternal lizard" because its fossil remains were found near a mud nest containing fifteen baby hadrosaurs, and so it is presumed to be the mother. The scientist who found this dinosaur believes that its nearness to the nest gives evidence that hadrosaurs took some care of their young.

Maiasaura is estimated to have been about 30 feet (9 m) long and stood 15 feet (4.5 m) high on its two strong, powerful legs. *Maiasaura* was a rather primitive duckbill. In appearance it is midway between the European *Iguanodon* and an American hadrosaur. The head was flat, with no crest.

The bowl-shaped nest had been made in the mud of an ancient riverbank. It measured a little over 6 feet (1.8 m) across and 2½ feet (75 cm) deep. The babies, which were nearly 3 feet (90 cm) long and 12 inches (30 cm) high at the hips, were at least a month old. Their teeth were already worn down. This seems to indicate that they had been chewing either coarse vegetable matter or a lot of gritty sand along with water plants from the river bottom. Their mother may have taken the young from the nest to feed during the daytime, then returned with them to the nest at night.

It is not known what catastrophe killed *Maiasaura* and its brood. Perhaps an erupting volcano covered them with ash, or maybe a mud slide buried them.

Maiasaura babies

PROSAUROLOPHUS
"First Crested Lizard"

Prosaurolophus (pro-sawr-OL-uh-fus) was the earliest of the crested duckbills in North America as far as we know. This rare animal lived in the early part of Late Cretaceous times along with *Hadrosaurus* and *Brachylophosaurus.*

The body and skull were similar to those of *Anatosaurus,* but *Prosaurolophus* had the beginning of a crest which rose like low knobs above the eyes. The crest was solid and ended in a short spike which pointed to the rear. The bill was smaller, shorter, and not so widely flared as that of *Anatosaurus,* which evolved millions of years later.

Prosaurolophus was probably a plains dweller. Its bones were found in Alberta, Canada.

Prosaurolophus

Saurolophus

SAUROLOPHUS
"Crested Lizard"

The first complete dinosaur skeleton found in Canada was a *Saurolophus* (sawr-OL-uh-fus). This duckbill probably was a descendant of *Prosaurolophus*. It lived several million years later, during the middle of the Late Cretaceous.

Saurolophus browsed on the shores of bayous alongside *Edmontosaurus*. Its body resembled that of *Edmontosaurus*, but the head was broader and the beak more spoon-shaped. A long, spike-like crest curved upward over the top of the skull. Like the crest of *Prosaurolophus*, this crest was solid. *Saurolophus* was smaller than *Edmontosaurus*, measuring 22 feet (6.5 m) long and standing 17 feet (5 m) high.

This plant eater may have browsed in herds. Herding would have provided some protection against their worst enemy, *Albertosaurus (Gorgosaurus)*. *Saurolophus* skeletons have been found in Alberta, Canada, along with those of hundreds of other dinosaurs. *Parksosaurus, Pachyrhinosaurus,* and "ostrich dinosaurs" were neighbors.

CORYTHOSAURUS
"Helmet Lizard"

Corythosaurus (ko-RITH-uh-sawr-us) was a hollow-crested hadrosaur that lived in western Canada during the early part of the Late Cretaceous. It was one of the more common dinosaurs of that period. A medium-sized duckbill, it grew to be 26–30 feet (8–9 m) long and weighed 2–3 tons (1.8–2.7 metric tons) when adult.

Its long, narrow head had a high, hollow, helmet-shaped, thin crest that capped the entire skull behind the beak. Air passages ran from the nostrils, which were low on the beak, up into the crest. There they made a loop, then descended down into the back of the throat. This crest may have improved the sense of smell, or it may have been used as a sex symbol (males having larger crests than females). Or it may have allowed the animal to breathe while eating constantly (its teeth suggest that it spent a lot of time eating). Some scientists think the crest may have been used as a resonating chamber to make the voice louder. If this was true, the noise near the Cretaceous riverbanks must have been deafening!

Corythosaurus was a bipedal animal with a flexible goose-like neck. It had a narrow, slightly arched back with a low, smooth ridge running down the center to a deep, narrow tail. The legs were large and powerful, but the forelimbs were short and slender.

Impressions left in Cretaceous sand show that this dinosaur's skin was covered with small polygonal bumps, giving it a pebbled surface similar to that of a football. Rows of larger, oval bumps covered the belly and pelvic area. Folds of skin hung down across the chest.

The beak of *Corythosaurus* was narrow and less ducklike than that of *Anatosaurus.* The teeth, however, were typically hadrosaurian. This graceful

Corythosaurus

animal probably browsed in large groups on ferns and leaves of young trees along riverbanks.

Corythosaurus had few defenses against its enemies, *Albertosaurus (Gorgosaurus),* and *Daspletosaurus.* Perhaps it had developed keen senses of hearing and smell and fled when it sensed the approach of an enemy.

Corythosaurus fossils have been found in Baja California as well as in western Canada. Hadrosaur neighbors of *Corythosaurus* were *Hadrosaurus, Lambeosaurus, Brachylophosaurus,* and *Parasaurolophus.* Dromaeosaurs and several kinds of armored and horned dinosaurs also lived nearby.

Skeletons of many young hadrosaurs have been found. One, named *Procheneosaurus* (pro-KEEN-ee-uh-sawr-us), was 11 feet (3.3 m) long. Its skull, which was 14 inches (35 cm) long, was topped with a hollow, humplike crest. Some scientists now believe that this dinosaur was a young *Corythosaurus.*

LAMBEOSAURUS
"Lambe's Lizard"

Lambeosaurus (LAM-be-uh-sawr-us) was named in honor of the Canadian paleontologist Lawrence Lambe. It was the first crested hadrosaur found in North America, and appears to have been as abundant as *Corythosaurus* along Late Cretaceous riverbanks and seashores. It probably browsed on higher vegetation than did *Corythosaurus.* This large duckbill may have been the largest known ornithischian, reaching 40 feet (12 m) or more in length.

The crest of this magnificent animal looks like a combination of those of *Corythosaurus* and *Saurolophus.* Like *Corythosaurus,* it had a large, hollow crest on the top of its skull. This crest was hatchet-shaped, and a sort of accessory spike or rod similar to the crest of *Saurolophus* pointed backward beyond the skull, forming a "handle" for the "hatchet."

The narrow nose ended in a broad, blunt beak. The body, though larger, was similar to that of *Saurolophus,* but *Lambeosaurus*'s legs were shorter and more powerful. The skin was similar to that of *Corythosaurus,*

113

but it apparently didn't have the larger tubercles (bumps) found on *Corythosaurus*.

Lambeosaurus fossils have been found in both Alberta, Canada, and Baja California in the same general areas where *Corythosaurus* has been found.

A few bones of an even larger hadrosaur were found in Baja California. This duckbill, the largest hadrosaur found so far, is estimated to be over 50 feet (15 m) long. It will not be assigned to a genus until more remains are found, but it was probably closely related to *Lambeosaurus*.

Lambeosaurus

HYPACROSAURUS
"High-ridged Lizard"

Hypacrosaurus (high-PAK-ruh-sawr-us) lived during the middle of the Late Cretaceous period. This large duckbill resembled its ancestor *Corythosaurus* in many ways. However, the hollow crest was larger and less rounded. The head measured 22 inches (55 cm) from the base of the skull to the top of the crest. The air passages through the crest were completely enclosed in bone.

An average adult *Hypacrosaurus* measured 25–30 feet (7.5–9 m) from the tip of the beak to the end of the tail. Like all hadrosaurs, it was bipedal, except possibly when feeding, and probably walked with the tail outstretched. The back arched slightly upward from the hips to the base of the neck. *Hypacrosaurus* has been compared to a gigantic turkey with a long tail like a crocodile's. The spines along its backbone were very long, giving it a high ridge down the back—and the reason for its name.

Hypacrosaurus

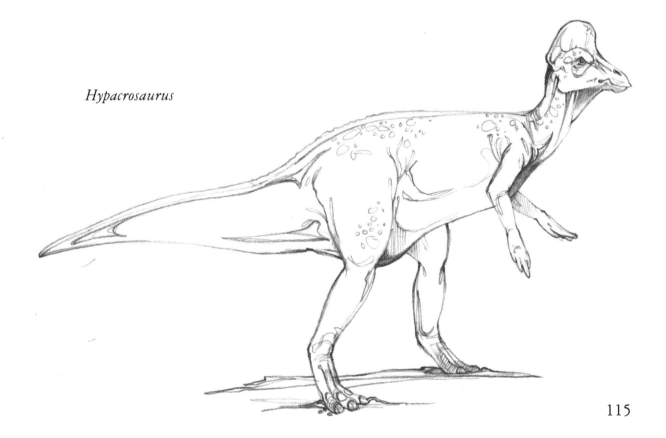

The arms and legs of *Hypacrosaurus* were longer than those of *Corythosaurus*. That suggests it was a good runner, and speed was perhaps its best defense against *Daspletosaurus* and *Albertosaurus (Gorgosaurus)*.

Hypacrosaurus was the most abundant animal in what is now Baja California during the middle part of Late Cretaceous times. It also inhabited the broadleaf forests of Late Cretaceous Alberta, Canada. A neighbor of *Edmontosaurus* and *Saurolophus*, it probably ate shrubs and ferns at a different height from those animals, perhaps 7–8 feet (2–2.5 m) above the ground.

A small hadrosaur found in Alberta, Canada, was given the name *Cheneosaurus* (KEEN-ee-uh-sawr-us). This animal had a rather large skull with a low, hollow crest similar to that of *Procheneosaurus*. Some authorities consider *Cheneosaurus* and *Procheneosaurus* to be the same. Others believe this dinosaur was a juvenile *Hypacrosaurus* or *Lambeosaurus*.

PARASAUROLOPHUS
"Similar-crested Lizard"

Parasaurolophus (par-uh-sawr-OL-uh-fus) first appeared in North America at the beginning of the Late Cretaceous period. It was one of the most remarkable of all the crested dinosaurs. Its crest was a long, hornlike tube that curved backward from the head to well beyond the shoulders. This extraordinary crest was twice as long as the animal's skull! Some measured as much as 5 feet (1.5 m) long.

All of the air *Parasaurolophus* breathed had to go through this crest. Air passages extended from the nostrils to the tip of the hollow tube and then doubled back again before going into the windpipe and lungs. The purpose of this tube is not known. It was once thought to be a snorkel, but it has no opening at the end. Some scientists think that its purpose was to improve the sense of smell. *Parasaurolophus* probably needed an extra-good sense of smell because it had no defense weapons to use against the large carnosaurs of that period. Whatever the purpose of the crest, it must have been a very successful design. *Parasaurolophus* lived to the end of the Cretaceous period, longer than any other hadrosaur.

Parasaurolophus was 30 feet (9 m) long and stood 16 feet (about 5 m)

116

high in a partly erect position. It weighed 3 or 4 tons (2.7 or 3.6 metric tons). Like all other hadrosaurs, it was bipedal and had a thick body with strong, heavy legs, and hoofed toes. The forelimbs were short and had webbed fingers.

This harmless dinosaur probably ate tough plant materials—pine needles or oak and poplar leaves—as well as fruit and seeds. It may have fed with numerous other hadrosaurs of different kinds on the outer edges of Late Cretaceous forests. Its ducklike beak was shaped like a scoop, which leads some scientists to believe it may sometimes have eaten succulent weeds from shallow water. Behind the beak were several rows of closely packed crushing and grinding teeth. As old teeth wore out, they were replaced by new ones. *Parasaurolophus* may have cut as many as ten to twenty thousand teeth in its lifetime!

Besides its keen sense of smell, *Parasaurolophus* had especially good hearing and sight. It may have been a good swimmer and a reasonably fast runner. The herds in which it browsed were ever alert to danger. At the first alarm, they turned and ran, or perhaps took to water.

Parasaurolophus has been found in New Mexico and Alberta, Canada.

Parasaurolophus

ANKYLOSAURUS
"Curved Lizard"

Ankylosaurus (ang-KILE-uh-sawr-us) is probably the best-known of the armored dinosaurs. This reptilian "tank" was 17 feet (5 m) long, 6 feet (1.8 m) wide, and a little over 4 feet (1.2 m) high. It weighed about 5 tons (4.5 metric tons).

The triangular-shaped head was 27 inches (68 cm) long and very broad. Thick spikes of bone resembling ears projected outward behind the eyes, making the head look even broader. The heavy jaws ended in a horny beak, and were filled with tiny, weak teeth in the back. Short, massive legs supported the broad, dome-shaped body. All four feet were short and broad. The toes were hoofed.

Ankylosaurus was well protected with armor made of thick oval plates of bone set close together in leathery skin. This armor covered the head, neck, back, and tail. Even the eyelids were protected by curved bony plates. A row of short spikes protected either side of the body, and the short, thick tail ended in a bony club.

When attacked, this slow-moving animal simply squatted to the ground. A predator couldn't have turned it over. The armor was adequate protection. However, if needed, the clublike tail was a good weapon. It could have broken an enemy's leg.

This peaceful plant eater lived in western North America until the end of the Cretaceous period. Its fossils have been found in the same areas as those of "ostrich dinosaurs," duckbills, and great horned dinosaurs. *Ankylosaurus* also lived alongside *Albertosaurus (Gorgosaurus)* and *Tyrannosaurus.*

Some writers use the name *Euoplocephalus* for this dinosaur because it was once believed to be the same, and that name is older. However, recent authorities on ankylosaurs consider them to be two different animals.

Ankylosaurus

PANOPLOSAURUS
"Armored Lizard"

Some scientists consider *Panoplosaurus* and *Edmontonia* to be the same animal and use the name *Panoplosaurus* (pan-OP-luh-sawr-us) because it is older. Others do not agree. Even if they are not the same, however, they are similar. *Edmontonia* (ed-mon-TONE-ee-uh) was named for the Edmonton rock formation in Alberta, Canada, where it was found.

These ankylosaurs were abundant in western North America around the beginning of Late Cretaceous times. Like all armored dinosaurs, they were quadrupedal and had short, stubby legs with hoofed feet. Rows of large bony plates, or scutes, covered the neck, back, tail, and head, which in *Edmontonia* was only 16 inches (40 cm) long. The throat was shielded by small round bones embedded in the skin. Long, heavy spikes protected the sides and shoulder region, but the tail was clubless. The largest of the spikes curved forward over the shoulders to protect the neck.

The pear-shaped heads were protected by heavy ridges of bone above the eyes. The animals had square, horny beaks and weak teeth. They probably ate soft plants such as ferns, lilies, arum, and cattails that grew along the riverbanks where they browsed. The nostrils were quite large, so they may have had a good sense of smell. This would have been useful in detecting the approach of an enemy.

120   *Panoplosaurus (Edmontonia)*

Panoplosaurus was a massive animal 15 feet (4.5 m) long and weighing up to 3 tons (2.7 metric tons). Its armor and its strength were its defense against predators. Like other ankylosaurs, it probably squatted to the ground when attacked.

These ankylosaurs have been found in Montana, South Dakota, Texas, and Alberta, Canada, along with *Corythosaurus, Lambeosaurus,* and *Albertosaurus.*

Some writers use the name *Paleoscincus* (pay-lee-o-SKINK-us) for this dinosaur because it was once believed to be the same, and this name is much older. However, recent authorities believe that *Paleoscincus,* which is known only from a single tooth, was a different ankylosaur.

EUOPLOCEPHALUS
"Well-protected Head"

Also called *Scolosaurus* (SKOLE-uh-sawr-us), "thorn lizard," *Euoplocephalus* (you-op-luh-SEF-uh-lus), the older name, is the correct one, as these two are now considered to be the same dinosaur.

This Late Cretaceous ankylosaur lived a few million years later than its cousin *Panoplosaurus.* It was more advanced and more heavily armored than its ancestor *Nodosaurus.*

The upper part of the body, from the nose to the tail, was covered with bony plates studded with rows of horny spikes projecting upward. These 4–6 inch (10–15 cm) spikes appeared at regular intervals, the largest being over the shoulders. The heavy tail was short and fat, ending in a bony knob with two long spikes. The eyes were well protected by bony projections. Only the belly of this animal was unprotected.

This enormous plant eater grew to be 18 feet (about 5.5 m) long and 8 feet (2.5 m) wide. It weighed up to 3½ tons (3.15 metric tons). *Euoplocephalus* was a slow animal and, like all ankylosaurs, walked on four short, stout legs. This animal must have eaten soft ground plants, for the head was carried low and the teeth were small and weak.

When threatened by danger, *Euoplocephalus* tucked its legs underneath

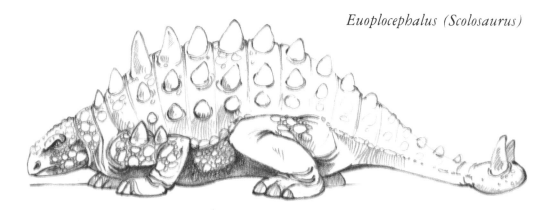

its body and squatted to the ground. It would have been impossible to turn it over. The tail was an effective weapon if needed.

Euoplocephalus probably browsed in dry uplands, away from the marshy swamps, where the ground was firm and the food plentiful.

Fossils of this dinosaur have been found in Alberta, Canada, in the same regions as those of *Albertosaurus (Gorgosaurus)* and several kinds of hadrosaurs.

Dyoplosaurus (die-OP-luh-sawr-us) and *Anodontosaurus* (an-uh-don-tuh-SAWR-us) are names given to fossil remains of two ankylosaurs that are now considered to be the same as *Euoplocephalus.* Both were found in Alberta, Canada.

Ceratopsians "Horned Face"

Ceratopsians (sair-uh-TOP-see-ans), the horned dinosaurs, were the last group of dinosaurs to evolve. They first appeared near the beginning of the Late Cretaceous period. Although their near ancestors, *Psittacosaurus* (SIT-a-ko-sawr-us), a parrot-beaked Mongolian ornithopod, and *Protoceratops* (pro-to-SAIR-uh-tops), the first true ceratopsian, have not been found in North America, they may have lived here. Many varieties evolved from this first stock. Nearly all of them have been found in North America.

These dinosaurs were ornithischian (bird-hipped) rather than saurischian (lizard-hipped). They were quadrupedal plant eaters with rhinoceros-like bodies and short, stocky tails. Their legs were short, with four toes on the hind feet and five on the forefeet.

The most distinctive features of ceratopsians were their horns and the bony frills that grew on the backs of their heads. The purpose of these frills was to provide a place for attachment of the neck and jaw muscles. Ceratopsian heads were large and heavy. As the skulls and horns grew larger, the frills grew larger to help support them. Baby ceratopsians did not have well-developed frills.

The horns were used as defense weapons. Both males and females had horns on their noses and above the eyes. Babies, however, were hornless.

When hatched, the young were small and helpless. They may have received some parental care until they were large enough to keep up with the herd. A ceratopsian nest with unhatched eggs and several young hatchlings was found in Mongolia. The nest is believed to belong to the small Mongolian *Protoceratops* whose skeleton was found nearby. The eggs in this nest were about 6 inches (15 cm) long. They had rough, wrinkled shells. Eighteen eggs arranged in three circles, one within another, had been laid in the sand nest.

The parrot-beaked ceratopsians had powerful jaws and strong cheek muscles. They probably ate twigs and branches. The back jaws were lined with layered rows of dozens of fast-growing teeth that chopped the food like a scissors, rather than crushing or grinding it. The teeth were replaced as rapidly as they wore out.

Vast numbers of these ornithischians roamed wooded uplands of western North America. These successful dinosaurs lived to the end of the Mesozoic Era and were among the very last of the dinosaurs. They may have been warm-blooded. A few scientists believe they could gallop at considerable speeds, but others doubt this.

Three main branches of ceratopsians lived in North America. **Protoceratopsians** were the earliest. They were small in size and had either no horns or very small ones. Two of these have been found in North America. **Short-frilled ceratopsians** had frills that did not cover their shoulders. The nose horns were long in some and short in others. Six short-frilled ceratopsians have been found in North America. The **long-frilled ceratopsians** had short horns on their noses and long ones above their eyes. Their frills extended back over their shoulders and had openings in them to reduce their weight. Five long-frilled ceratopsians have been found on the North American continent.

LEPTOCERATOPS
"Slender-horned Face"

This protoceratopsian, the most primitive horned dinosaur known, has been found only in North America. It is closely related to the Mongolian *Protoceratops.* Although the only *Leptoceratops* fossils found so far were in rock from the latest part of the Cretaceous, a few paleontologists speculate that this dinosaur lived during the entire Late Cretaceous period. Some scientists call it a throwback to *Psittacosaurus.* However, not everyone agrees.

Leptoceratops (lep-tuh-SAIR-uh-tops) had no horns, even though the name means "slender-horned face." *Leptoceratops* was slim and lightly built. It was pig-sized, weighing about 500 pounds (225 kg) and measuring about 6 feet (1.8 m) long and 2½ feet (75 cm) high.

Its large, deep head had a narrow snout that ended in a strong, curved, parrotlike beak. The back of the head flared into a short, solid frill that did not cover its short neck.

Leptoceratops had a short tail, but the legs were relatively long and slender. The forelegs, which were much shorter than the hind legs, had five short toes. The back feet had four toes, which were clawed instead of hoofed. *Leptoceratops* may occasionally have run on its hind legs, but it usually walked on all fours.

Leptoceratops

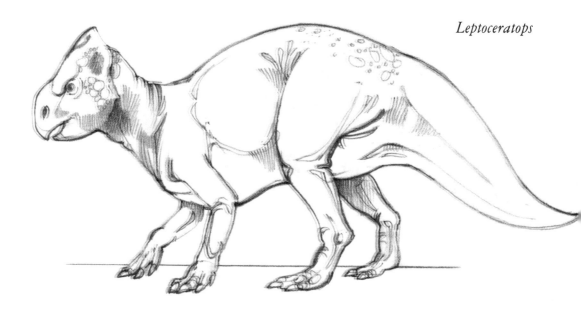

124

This peaceful plant eater may have roamed forested areas, maybe in large herds, browsing on low-level vegetation. When danger approached, it probably turned and ran, for it had no other means of defense.

Leptoceratops existed alongside herds of hadrosaurs, *Triceratops, Ankylosaurus, Tyrannosaurus,* and *Alamosaurus.* Other creatures also shared its environment—giant monitor lizards, opossums, and squirrel-like mammals.

Leptoceratops fossils have been found only in Alberta, Canada.

MONTANACERATOPS
"Montana's Horned Face"

Montanaceratops (mon-TAN-uh-sair-uh-tops) was also a protoceratopsian. This dinosaur was a close relative of both *Leptoceratops* and the Mongolian *Protoceratops,* but was more advanced than either. *Montanaceratops* more closely resembled ceratopsians. It had a well-developed, but small, horn on the nose, and the bony frill that covered its neck, like the frill of *Protoceratops,* had holes through the bone. However, the frill of *Montanaceratops* was larger than the frill of either *Protoceratops* or *Leptoceratops.* The head was smaller than that of *Leptoceratops* and the front legs were longer. The tail was somewhat heavier.

Montanaceratops was named for the state of Montana, where its fossils

Montanaceratops

were found. It lived alongside *Pachyrhinosaurus, Albertosaurus,* and huge numbers of hadrosaurs.

This small protoceratopsian lived in the early part of Late Cretaceous times, but failed to survive into the last part of the Cretaceous.

MONOCLONIUS
"Single-horned"

Monoclonius (mon-o-CLONE-ee-us) was one of the first of the true ceratopsians in North America. This horned dinosaur was a member of the short-frilled group. Its size had increased three times over that of its ancestor, *Protoceratops. Monoclonius* may have weighed eight times as much, perhaps 2½–3 tons (2.25–2.7 metric tons). It measured 18–20 feet (5.5–6 m) long and stood about 6 feet (1.8 m) tall at the shoulders.

Although the frill is considered short, the huge head was 5–6 feet (1.5–1.8 m) from its parrotlike beak to the end of its knob-edged frill. Large holes in the bone of the frill lightened its weight. A very long, straight horn grew on the nose of *Monoclonius.* Only small stumps decorated the brows. The nose horn was a defense weapon. *Monoclonius* charged its enemies and stabbed them with the horn.

The body of *Monoclonius* was typically ceratopsian, massive and very rhinoceros-like. The tail was relatively short and bulky. This four-footed animal may have run or galloped in the same manner as hoofed animals of today, although some scientists dispute this.

Large numbers of this peaceful plant eater roamed throughout western North America in the early part of Late Cretaceous times. They were well protected from predators by their long horns and speed.

Another, very similar dinosaur, *Centrosaurus* (SEN-truh-sawr-us), looked almost exactly like *Monoclonius* except that the nose horn of *Centrosaurus* curved forward. Some scientists think they are the same. Others believe they are different genera. *Centrosaurus*'s nose horn was 18 inches (45 cm) long. Its knobbed frill had two small hooked spikes in the center at the edge.

Five young, 6-foot (1.8-m), single-horned dinosaurs were found in

Monoclonius

Montana and named *Brachyceratops* (brak-ee-SAIR-uh-tops). These animals are now believed to be young *Centrosaurus* or *Monoclonius*. Five half-grown ceratopsians found together suggests to some scientists that the young animals may have received some kind of care from their parents.

Eoceratops (EE-o-sair-uh-tops) is a name given to a similar species of ceratopsian.

STYRACOSAURUS
"Spiked Lizard"

Styracosaurus (sty-RAK-uh-sawr-us) was a short-frilled ceratopsian that lived in North America at the same time as *Monoclonius*.

Like all ceratopsians, *Styracosaurus* was a quadrupedal plant eater with a bulky body and a short, thick tail. The feet were short and broad, with hoofed toes.

This dinosaur was 18 feet (about 5.5 m) long and 6 feet (1.8 m) tall at the shoulders. It weighed around 3 tons (2.7 metric tons). The head was enormous. A horn nearly 2 feet (60 cm) long and 6 inches (15 cm) thick grew on the nose, but only stumps grew above the eyes. Instead of brow

Styracosaurus

horns, this ceratopsian had six long spikes along the upper edge of the frill, which was 4-feet (1.2-m) wide. These spikes pointed backward over the shoulders, with the two center spikes extending farthest back. The frill itself covered only the neck.

Styracosaurus ate low, bushy, shrublike plants that it snipped off with a sharp beak and chopped with strong cheek teeth. This dinosaur may have roamed the open uplands of western North America in large numbers. When threatened by danger, *Styracosaurus* probably charged its attacker at speeds up to 20 miles (32 km) per hour—some say even 30 miles (48 km) per hour.

It may have shared its environment with *Albertosaurus* and numerous crested hadrosaurs. *Styracosaurus* fossils have been found in western Canada.

PACHYRHINOSAURUS
"Thick-nosed Lizard"

Pachyrhinosaurus (PAK-ee-rine-o-sawr-us), a short-frilled ceratopsian of the Late Cretaceous, was a relative of *Monoclonius* and *Styracosaurus,* but lived several million years later. Its body was quite similar, but *Pachyrhinosaurus* was larger than its relatives, measuring about 20 feet (6 m) long and weighing around 4 tons (3.6 metric tons).

Instead of horns, *Pachyrhinosaurus* had a thick, pear-shaped bony plate on its nose above its large nostrils and in front of the eyes. This plate was 22 inches (55 cm) long and 14 inches (35 cm) wide. It was rough and slightly cratered, like a volcano. The rim of the crater was nearly 5 inches (13 cm) high. Similar, but smaller, fist-sized knobs of bone grew above each eye.

Its huge skull was as large as that of *Monoclonius.* The frill was wide, but the face was short, with a broad nose. Like *Styracosaurus, Pachyrhinosaurus* had spikes along the back edge of its short frill. Although the spikes were shorter than those of *Styracosaurus,* some were up to 9 inches (23 cm) long.

This animal probably browsed in forested marshlands and may have

Pachyrhinosaurus

herded with others of its kind for protection from *Albertosaurus*. However, *Pachyrhinosaurus* probably did not feed with other kinds of ceratopsians. *Pachyrhinosaurus* fossils have been found in Alberta, Canada.

CHASMOSAURUS
"Open Lizard"

The first of the long-frilled ceratopsians, *Chasmosaurus* (KAZ-muh-sawr-us) lived during the early part of Late Cretaceous times, along with *Monoclonius*. This cousin of *Monoclonius* may have been the ancestor of all other long-frilled ceratopsians. *Chasmosaurus* was one of the most common ceratopsians of its time.

This dinosaur resembled a rhinoceros and probably even ran like one. However, *Chasmosaurus* had a neck frill, and its tail was much longer and heavier than a rhino's. It's name refers to openings in its neck frill. *Chas-*

mosaurus was a medium-sized ceratopsian, about 16 feet (5 m) long. It probably weighed 2½ tons (2.25 metric tons).

Chasmosaurus had a small nose horn, but two moderately long horns projected from its brow with a slight backward curve. The very long frill, or neck shield, stretched back over the neck and shoulders. Very large openings went through the frill bones on each side, but they did not go through the skin and muscle covering. The name of this dinosaur refers to these openings.

The front legs of this quadruped were short, so the head was carried close to the ground. *Chasmosaurus* probably ate low ground plants, cropping them with its hard horny beak and chopping and slicing, rather than grinding or crushing, with its teeth. The jaws and bite were powerful, and it is possible that the beak as well as the horns was used as a weapon.

Skin impressions show that the skin of *Chasmosaurus* was covered with rows of very large buttonlike scales, or tubercles. Some of these were 2 inches (5 cm) in diameter. They were set in a background of small scales. Alternating rows of large scales ran from the neck to the tail. The rows were about 5 inches (13 cm) apart.

Chasmosaurus has been found in western Canada. Other dinosaurs that lived at the same time were *Lambeosaurus, Albertosaurus, Corythosaurus, Daspletosaurus,* and *Dromaeosaurus.*

Chasmosaurus

ANCHICERATOPS
"Similar Horned Face"

This long-frilled ceratopsian closely resembled its probable ancestor, *Chasmosaurus,* and replaced that dinosaur about the middle of Late Cretaceous times. *Anchiceratops* (ANG-kee-sair-uh-tops) had three horns—a short, stubby one on its nose and two relatively large ones above the eyes. The forward-pointing brow horns were long and slender.

The body of *Anchiceratops* was longer than that of *Chasmosaurus,* but the tail was a little shorter. The long neck shield was decorated with triangular-shaped projections along the back edge. The holes in the shield bones were smaller than those in the frill of *Chasmosaurus.*

Anchiceratops roamed along the stream banks of Late Cretaceous coastal plains in what is now Alberta, Canada. It probably ate ferns and other ground plants. It may have pushed over fern trees to get at the tender leaves on top.

Anchiceratops

Edmontosaurus, Hypacrosaurus, Struthiomimus, Dromiceiomimus, and *Albertosaurus* all lived in the same region as *Anchiceratops.* Its size, moderate speed, and horns were adequate protection for *Anchiceratops* against the predators.

ARRHINOCERATOPS
"Without a Nose-horn Face"

This relative of *Chasmosaurus* lived during the same period as *Anchiceratops* and resembled that dinosaur. *Arrhinoceratops* (ah-RINE-o-sair-uh-tops) was about the same size and had a similarly small nose horn. However, the forward-pointing brow horns of *Arrhinoceratops* were longer and more curved than those of *Anchiceratops.*

The long neck shield of *Arrhinoceratops* may have been armed with spikes instead of triangular projections. The shield had quite small openings. *Arrhinoceratops*'s short, high snout ended in a short, horny beak.

Fossils of this dinosaur have been found in Alberta, Canada.

Arrhinoceratops

PENTACERATOPS
"Five-horned Face"

Pentaceratops (PEN-tuh-sair-uh-tops) had an extremely long frill, or neck shield. It extended far back over the shoulders for more than a third of the length of the long, heavy body. The skull of *Pentaceratops* measured 7½ feet (2.25 m) from the beak to the end of the shield. The body, including the head and a relatively short tail, was only 20 feet (6 m) long. The frill was deeply scalloped along the edges and had very large openings in the bone.

This long-frilled ceratopsian was similar to its ancestor, *Chasmosaurus.* It had a short nose horn and long horns above the eyes. However, the brow horns of *Pentaceratops* were larger and longer than those of *Chasmosaurus.* In addition, *Pentaceratops* had two long, hornlike growths on the shield near the corners of the jaws, giving it a total of five horns.

This four-legged plant eater may have charged attackers at a 20 mph (32 kph) gallop, like a rhinoceros. Although there is no evidence of herding in this animal, some scientists think *Pentaceratops* may have roamed, like buffalo, throughout western North America. Its fossils have been found in New Mexico and Alberta, Canada. It lived during the same time period as *Anchiceratops* and *Arrhinoceratops.*

Pentaceratops

134

TOROSAURUS
"Piercing Lizard"

Torosaurus (TOR-o-sawr-us) had the longest neck shield of all the ceratopsians. One of the last of the horned dinosaurs to develop, *Torosaurus* took the place of all other long-frilled ceratopsians during the very last of Late Cretaceous times.

This large dinosaur was 20 feet (6 m) long and may have weighed around 4 or 5 tons (3.6 or 4.5 metric tons). The body was typically ceratopsian, but *Torosaurus* had a longer skull than any other known land animal. The skull measured 8½ feet (about 2.5 m) from the tip of the horny beak to the back edge of the shield. This enormous shield was flat and rectangular. It was 5½ feet (about 1.5 m) across and extended well beyond the shoulders. However, the frill openings were much smaller than those of *Pentaceratops.*

A small horn grew on *Torosaurus's* nose, but the large, forward-pointing brow horns were 2 feet (60 cm) long and extended beyond the snout. Its name refers to these formidable horns.

Tyrannosaurus was probably the greatest enemy of *Torosaurus,* but *Torosaurus* was well protected. This ceratopsian may have browsed in large herds. It probably ate lower vegetation than most other plant eaters of the time. This dinosaur lived during the same time period as *Triceratops, Ankylosaurus,* and *Anatosaurus.* Its fossils have been found in Wyoming and Alberta, Canada.

TRICERATOPS
"Three-horned Face"

Triceratops (try-SAIR-uh-tops) was the largest and heaviest of the horned dinosaurs. This ceratopsian's immense head alone was longer than *Leptoceratops.* The massive body was four times longer and eighteen times heavier than that dinosaur. *Triceratops* measured 25 feet (7.5 m) from the

Torosaurus

end of its snout to the tip of its short, heavy tail. It stood 9½ feet (about 3 m) tall and weighed about 5–6 tons (4.5–5.4 metric tons)—almost as much as an adult elephant. But it was not as tall as an elephant.

The skull measured 7 feet (about 2 m) from the tip of the long nose to the edge of the frill, or neck shield. This broad, saddle-shaped shield extended back over the neck to the shoulders. It was smooth and solid, with no holes through the bone such as those in the frills of long-frilled ceratopsians. The rear edge of the shield was slightly scalloped.

Triceratops had a short, thick nose horn and two enormous forward-pointing horns above the eyes. In some specimens these horns were 40 inches (1 m) long—as long as a broom handle!

Large numbers of this four-legged plant eater browsed the open plains, feeding upon the lush semitropical vegetation, possibly palms and cycads. They may have pushed over taller trees to get to the tender top branches. The branches were snipped off with sharp parrotlike beaks and chopped up with scissorlike teeth. The teeth dropped out and were replaced as soon as they became worn.

Triceratops probably had no real enemies. It was well protected by its enormous horns, its neck shield, and thick, leathery skin. *Tyrannosaurus* was no match for this animal. *Triceratops*'s brain was twice as large as that of *Tyrannosaurus,* and its eyes were quite large, indicating keen eyesight. It has been estimated that this dinosaur could run 30 miles (48 km) per hour, but this has been challenged. *Triceratops*'s legs were short, thick, and strong, but not designed for high speed.

Triceratops was an aggressive animal. Some fossil shields bear horn scars. Perhaps it fought with others of its kind to defend its home territory or to win a mate.

Triceratops fossils have been found in Montana, Wyoming, and Alberta, Canada. This successful animal developed late in the Mesozoic Era. Great numbers lived in North America toward the end of Late Cretaceous times. One of the very last of the dinosaurs to die out, *Triceratops* lived about 5 million years—then suddenly it, too, became extinct. Afterward there were no more dinosaurs.

Triceratops

6

The Mystery of Dinosaur Extinction

What caused the dinosaurs to disappear suddenly without a trace? No one knows for sure. We may never know unless a time machine is invented. Many scientists have studied the problem and many theories have been given for this mass extinction.

The extinction was sudden, but it didn't happen in a single day. Some scientists think it may have happened in a single year. Others think it took hundreds or even thousands of years for the last of the dinosaurs to become extinct. Many believe it occurred over several million years. However, in terms of geological time even this is rather sudden.

Whatever happened seems to have happened all over the world. It affected many different forms of life, both on land and in the sea. Large numbers of living species became extinct along with *Triceratops* and *Tyrannosaurus*. Half of the flowering plants; many kinds of mammals; several kinds of plankton (microscopic sea plants and animals); the dinosaurs' flying cousins, pterosaurs; the big sea reptiles, plesiosaurs and mosasaurs; floating shellfish called ammonites; and all of the dinosaurs vanished from the face of the earth. Why were all these wiped out? Why did other species, such as opossums, crocodiles, turtles, lizards, and snakes, survive?

One theory is that dinosaurs died of old age. Perhaps their adaptive powers simply wore out. Their extinction took place at a time when great mountain ranges were being formed. These upheavals caused many changes to which dinosaurs would have had to adapt. However, they were gradual changes, and this theory does not explain why creatures that had been so very adaptable for millions of years suddenly lost their ability to adapt. It also completely ignores other extinctions.

Another theory suggests that dinosaur brains were too small. Dinosaurs were too stupid to adjust to the changing world, claim defenders of this theory. It is true that some (but not all) dinosaurs had the smallest brains in proportion to the size of their bodies of all known vertebrates. But their brains were large enough to serve adequately for 140 million years. That is much longer than humans with their huge brains have existed. The human race has lived only about one or two million years. Then, too, brain size is not a good measure of ability. Ants with pinhead-size brains can solve difficult problems. *Stenonychosaurus* and *Dromaeosaurus* were at least as smart as birds, yet they died out and birds didn't. Stupidity couldn't have caused plants and plankton to become extinct.

Another often heard theory is that the dinosaurs were killed off by the more intelligent and adaptable warm-blooded mammals. This is hardly possible. The mammals of the Cretaceous were very small—much too small to eat huge eggs. They had lived with the dinosaurs for 100 million years. Why hadn't they killed them off before the dinosaurs became so numerous? What about the sea life? Marine reptiles gave birth to their young alive. What killed them? What killed the plants?

Some scientists theorize that flowering plants killed dinosaurs. Plants may have contained certain poisons which dinosaurs couldn't taste, and when they ate enough, the plants killed them, according to this theory. But flowering plants could hardly have caused all the extinctions. Too, ornithopods had thrived on flowering plants for millions of years before the extinctions took place.

Still another theory says perhaps grasses evolved and covered the earth, displacing ferns. Dinosaurs didn't have the right kind of teeth to chew grass, so perhaps they starved to death. This theory leaves many unanswered questions. The earth's plants changed considerably during the Mesozoic Era. Dinosaurs had always been able to adapt to such changes. They actually increased enormously in numbers after flowering plants appeared. Why wouldn't they have adapted in the same way to grasses?

Another theory states that changes in the earth's surface were responsible for the death of the dinosaurs. We know the extinctions occurred at the same time the Rockies, Andes, Himalayas, and Alps were rising, and that the various continents had drifted apart and assumed approximately their present positions. Inland seas receded, swamps turned into dry uplands, and there was much volcanic action during the last ten thousand years of the Mesozoic.

Some scientists suggest that the volcanic activity destroyed the earth's ozone layer, allowing too much deadly ultraviolet radiation from the sun to reach the earth's surface. This theory seems plausible. However, these changes at the end of the era were less drastic than the changes that occurred during earlier parts of the Mesozoic, and dinosaurs survived those.

Other scientists theorize that it was climatic changes that killed the dinosaurs. Some suggest that seasons may have developed, with harsh, cold winters and very hot summers. Dinosaurs were unable to adjust to such extremes of temperature, so they say. The problem with this theory is that seasons actually began about the middle of the Late Cretaceous, some 15 to 20 million years before extinction.

Still other scientists think that a sharp drop in temperature occurred at the end of the Cretaceous, 65 million years ago. Perhaps this did in the dinosaurs. This theory has merit. Dinosaurs had no fur or feathers for insulation against the cold. They were too large to burrow in the ground. The nakedness of their skin could have caused their extinction. Small mammals and birds may have survived because they had fur and feathers. A drastic cooling of the seas would have caused plankton and ammonites to die, cutting off the food supply of the large marine reptiles.

But other scientists do not believe cooling alone caused all the extinctions. They think it must have been a much greater ecological disruption, something that caused great changes in the food supply. Animals that survived, such as opossums and birds, could hibernate or were very mobile. Plants that survived had seeds that could lie dormant for long periods. Drill cores taken from the ocean bottom suggest that something happened relatively suddenly to wipe out much of the surface-dwelling sea life around 65 million years ago.

What could cause such a sudden, worldwide disruption? One theory is that the receding seas reduced the amount of marine algae that absorb carbon dioxide, causing carbon dioxide to build up in the atmosphere. This, however, would cause the earth's temperature to rise, not fall. But huge dinosaurs had no insulation against the heat, just as they had none against cold. Proponents of this theory argue that extreme heat could have prevented dinosaur eggs from being fertilized. Large numbers of unhatched eggs have been found in Late Cretaceous rock, and perhaps they didn't hatch because they weren't fertilized. However, some scientists think they didn't hatch because their shells were much thinner than they had been in earlier times.

142

Others speculate that the disruption was caused by the spillover of a once-isolated freshwater Arctic ocean. When the continents broke apart, this Arctic water flooded the world's oceans, they say. This reduced the oceans' salinity and lowered their temperature. The problem with this theory is that there is no direct evidence the Arctic ocean ever was a freshwater ocean. As with all the other theories, there is no proof.

Another theory says that maybe a dense cloud of dust caused by a huge meteorite hitting the earth filtered the sun's energy and dimmed the sunlight, stunting plant growth and resulting in mass starvation. Yet another suggests that a huge comet fell into the ocean, heating the water and raising air temperature, but it is doubted that this would cause worldwide extinction.

Many scientists favor the theory that only a catastrophic event such as a supernova explosion could have caused all the extinctions. That kind of explosion happens frequently in the universe. When stars get very old they explode, sending out huge amounts of radiation. A star exploding near our solar system would cause tremendous amounts of X-rays and gamma rays to rain down on the earth. Scientists theorize that this may have happened at the end of Cretaceous times. If it did, the resulting high levels of X-rays in the atmosphere would have caused the temperature to drop. The temperature drop would have caused the death of plankton and ammonites that floated on the surface of the sea. Marine life that fed upon them would also have died. Radiation could have caused thinning of dinosaur egg shells. Modern birds lay eggs with thin shells when under environmental stress. Thin shells would have been too fragile to support the growing baby dinosaurs, and the eggs would not have hatched.

A recently proposed theory claims that it was an asteroid from within our solar system colliding with the earth that caused the extinction, instead of an exploding supernova. This theory is based on unusually high levels of iridium (a metallic element) found in clay sediments of that time taken from several different locations. Scientists proposing this theory say that only an iridium-containing asteroid could have deposited the kind and amount of iridium they found. They suggest that the collision caused a cloud of dust to circle the earth, blocking the sunlight for several years. All plants would have died. Only animals able to eat decaying vegetation would have survived. However, plants with seeds that could lie dormant for as much as ten years could grow again as soon as the dust cloud settled.

Another theory suggests that the widespread extinctions were caused by a reversal of the earth's magnetic poles caused by large wobbles in the earth's spin. Geological evidence shows that the earth's magnetic field has temporarily died out and reversed numerous times in the past—once about every fifty thousand to one million years. When the magnetic field is weak, the earth is exposed to high levels of radiation and ultraviolet light, which can cause genetic mutations. Ammonites and dinosaurs developed odd and unusual shapes in Late Cretaceous times. Just as hadrosaurs grew strange crests and ceratopsians grew outrageous frills, ammonites grew strangely shaped shells. Were they all victims of a reversal of the earth's magnetic poles?

We don't know. Perhaps a combination of these theories holds the answer. What we do know is that dinosaurs did not die out because they were huge, stupid, slow-moving animals. They were not. Neither were they mistakes of nature. All of them were very successful animals that lived several millions of years. Collectively, they ruled the earth for 140 million years. Then they were gone. Only their descendants, the birds, survived.

It was only after the dinosaurs disappeared that mammals were able to evolve and fill all of their niches.

Not enough is known about dinosaurs. Although we know a great deal about them, much more remains a secret locked in the past. Perhaps you will find the key.

For Further Reading

Charig, Alan J. *A New Look at the Dinosaurs.* New York: Mayflower Books, 1979.

Colbert, Edwin H. *The Age of Reptiles.* New York: W. W. Norton & Co., 1965.

————. *Dinosaurs, Their Discovery and Their World.* New York: E. P. Dutton & Co., 1961.

————. *The Year of the Dinosaur.* New York: Charles Scribner's Sons, 1977.

Desmond, Adrian J. *The Hot-Blooded Dinosaurs.* New York: Warner Books, 1977.

Fenton, Carroll Lane. *Tales Told by Fossils.* New York: Doubleday & Co., 1966.

Kurtén, Björn. *The Age of the Dinosaurs.* New York: McGraw-Hill, 1968.

Long, Robert A., and Welles, Samuel P. *All New Dinosaurs.* Santa Barbara: Bellerophon Books, 1975.

McIntosh, Johns. *Dinosaur National Monument.* Phoenix: Constellation Phoenix, Inc., 1977.

McLoughlin, John C. *Archosauria: A New Look at the Old Dinosaur.* New York: The Viking Press, 1979.

Moody, Richard. *A Natural History of Dinosaurs.* London: Chartwell, 1977.

————. *The World of Dinosaurs.* New York: Grosset & Dunlap, 1977.

Ostrom, John H. "A New Look at Dinosaurs." *National Geographic,* August 1978, pp. 152–85.

————. *The Strange World of Dinosaurs.* New York: G. P. Putnam's Sons, 1964.

Romer, Alfred Sherwood. *Vertebrate Paleontology.* Chicago: University of Chicago Press, 1966.

Russell, Dale A. *A Vanishing World.* Ottawa: National Museum of Natural Sciences, 1977.

Swinton, W. E. *The Dinosaurs.* New York: John Wiley & Sons–Interscience, 1970.

Tweedie, Michael. *The World of Dinosaurs.* New York: William Morrow & Co., 1977.

White, Theodore E. *Dinosaurs at Home.* New York: Vantage Press, 1968.

Reference, by Location, of North American Dinosaur Discoveries

Index, Including Illustrations